HELPING CHILDREN TO
MANAGE FRIENDSHIPS

Also part of the Helping Children to Build Wellbeing and Resilience series

Helping Children to Manage Anger
Photocopiable Activity Booklet to Support Wellbeing and Resilience
Deborah M. Plummer
Illustrated by Alice Harper
ISBN 978 1 78775 863 6
eISBN 978 1 78775 864 3

Helping Children to Manage Transitions
Photocopiable Activity Booklet to Support Wellbeing and Resilience
Deborah M. Plummer
Illustrated by Alice Harper
ISBN 978 1 78775 861 2
eISBN 978 1 78775 862 9

Helping Children to Manage Stress
Photocopiable Activity Booklet to Support Wellbeing and Resilience
Deborah M. Plummer
Illustrated by Alice Harper
ISBN 978 1 78775 865 0
eISBN 978 1 78775 866 7

Using Imagination, Mindful Play and Creative Thinking to Support Wellbeing and Resilience in Children
Deborah M. Plummer
Illustrated by Alice Harper
eISBN 978 1 78775 867 4

Helping Children to Build Communication Skills
Photocopiable Activity Booklet to Support Wellbeing and Resilience
Deborah M. Plummer
Illustrated by Alice Harper
ISBN 978 1 78775 870 4
eISBN 978 1 78775 871 1

Helping Children to Build Self-Confidence
Photocopiable Activity Booklet to Support Wellbeing and Resilience
Deborah M. Plummer
Illustrated by Alice Harper
ISBN 978 1 78775 872 8
eISBN 978 1 78775 873 5

Helping Children *to* Manage Friendships

Photocopiable Activity Booklet to Support Wellbeing and Resilience

Deborah M. Plummer

Illustrations by Alice Harper

Jessica Kingsley Publishers
London and Philadelphia

First published in Great Britain in 2022 by Jessica Kingsley Publishers
An imprint of Hodder & Stoughton Ltd
An Hachette Company

Some material was first published in *Self-Esteem Games for Children* [2006], *Helping Children to Build Self-Esteem* [2007], *Social Skills Games for Children* [2008], *Helping Children to Improve Their Communication Skills* [2011], *Focusing and Calming Games for Children* [2012] and *Helping Adolescents and Adults to Build Self-Esteem* [2014]. This edition first published in Great Britain in 2022 by Jessica Kingsley Publishers.

1

A CIP catalogue record for this title is available from the British Library and the Library of Congress

ISBN 978 1 78775 868 1
eISBN 978 1 78775 869 8

Printed and bound in Great Britain by Bell & Bain Limited

Jessica Kingsley Publishers' policy is to use papers that are natural, renewable and recyclable products and made from wood grown in sustainable forests. The logging and manufacturing processes are expected to conform to the environmental regulations of the country of origin.

Jessica Kingsley Publishers
Carmelite House
50 Victoria Embankment,
London EC4Y 0DZ

www.jkp.com

Contents

Acknowledgements

I have collected or devised the games and activities in this series of books over a 30-year period of working first as a speech and language therapist with children and adults, and then as a lecturer and workshop facilitator. Some were contributed by children during their participation in therapy groups or by teachers and therapists during workshops and discussions. Thank you!

The suggestions for adaptations and the expansion activities have arisen from my experiences of running children's groups. Many of them combine elements of ImageWork (Dr Dina Glouberman), Personal Construct Theory (see, for example, Peggy Dalton and Gavin Dunnett) and Solution-Focused Brief Therapy (Insoo Kim Berg and Steve de Shazer). Thank you to my teachers and mentors in these fields.

I have also found the following books helpful:

- Arnold, A. (1976) *The World Book of Children's Games*. London: Pan Books Ltd.
- Beswick, C. (2003) *The Little Book of Parachute Play*. London: Featherstone Education Ltd.
- Brandes, D. and Phillips, H. (1979) *Gamesters' Handbook: 140 Games for Teachers and Group Leaders*. London: Hutchinson.
- Dunn, O. (1978) *Let's Play Asian Children's Games*. Macmillan Southeast Asia in association with the Asian Cultural Centre for UNESCO.
- Liebmann, M. (2004) *Art Therapy for Groups: A Handbook of Themes and Exercises* (2nd edition). London and New York: Routledge.
- Masheder, M. (1989) *Let's Play Together*. London: Green Print.
- Neelands, J. (1990) *Structuring Drama Work: A Handbook of Available Forms in Theatre and Drama*. Cambridge: Cambridge University Press.

Note: Please remember, if you are a parent or carer and you are concerned about ongoing and persistently high levels of anxiety or low mood in a child, it is always best to seek further support via your child's school or your child's doctor. This book is not intended as a substitute for the professional help that may be needed when children are experiencing clinically recognized difficulties, such as chronic school phobia, severe social anxiety or childhood depression.

Wherever 'wellbeing' is used without further specification, this refers to social, psychological and emotional wellbeing.

As with any games involving the use of equipment, the parachute games outlined in this book should be supervised by an adult at all times.

The following icons are used throughout to indicate the three elements of the IMPACT approach:

Imagination

Mindful Play

Creative Thinking

Introduction

This book is one of a series based on the use of Imagination (I), Mindful Play (MP) and Creative Thinking (CT) to enhance social, psychological and emotional wellbeing and resilience in children. IMPACT activities and strategies encourage children to build life skills through carefully structured and supportive play experiences. Emphasis is given to the important role played by adult facilitators in creating a safe space in which children can share and explore feelings and difficulties and experiment with different ways of thinking and 'being'. This approach is explained in the accompanying eBook *Using Imagination, Mindful Play and Creative Thinking to Support Wellbeing and Resilience in Children*, which also contains many further ideas for games and activities and examples of how the IMPACT approach can enhance daily interactions with children.

USING THIS BOOK

The games and activities in this book help children to:

- identify some of their worries and concerns about friendships
- identify their current strengths and skills
- develop or consolidate specific skills and strategies that will be useful for managing friendships and engagement with the wider community.

Facilitator involvement

All the games and activities in the Helping Children to Build Wellbeing and Resilience series offer opportunities for facilitators to take an active part. This is particularly relevant for this book, *Helping Children to Manage Friendships*. Our participation reflects the nature of extended communities and gives us an opportunity to have fun alongside the children. Throughout the games in this book, the term 'game coordinator' therefore refers to either adult or child participants, as appropriate for the level and stage of each group.

Activities

The first section of games and activities, 'IMPACT Essentials for Managing Friendships' (see section II), introduces children to the central features of the IMPACT approach – using imagery, being mindful and thinking creatively. There are also activities for group 'gelling' and for exploring relevant concepts such as self-respect and respect for others. Each book in this series has a different set of foundation activities. With a slight change of emphasis, you will be able to use any of these to supplement your sessions if needed.

The remainder of the sections are arranged in accordance with specific aspects of managing friendships: 'Being Part of a Group', 'Understanding Friendships', 'Cooperation and Negotiation' and 'Celebrating Together'. You might also find it useful to add a selection of games and activities from *Helping Children to Manage Anger*, which is available in this series. This looks at how we might help children to understand and manage strong emotions – an important aspect of negotiating friendships and building community skills.

The creative potential for supporting skill development is one of the wonderful features of childhood games. Play of this nature provides invaluable opportunities for children to learn through imitation, to experience the consequences of their actions and to experiment with different skills and different outcomes without fear of failure or being judged unfavourably by others.

The multi-faceted nature of games means that in almost every game played there will be chances to enhance basic life skills, which will, in turn, help children to negotiate a variety of situations now and in the future. For example, in this book, the emphasis on empathy, awareness of others, understanding different perspectives, recognizing, acknowledging and sharing feelings, negotiating and cooperating, problem-solving and effective communication skills such as active listening will all contribute to effective conflict resolution.

I have given several suggestions for specific skills that might be learned or further developed during each game and its associated activities, but these are not exhaustive. You may want to add more to suit your own focus of work.

Ideas are suggested for adaptations. These illustrate some of the many ways in which a basic game can be simplified or made more complex. This also means that IMPACT games and activities can be revisited several times, thus expanding each child's repertoire of appropriate skills and offering opportunities for choice and flexibility in how they initiate and participate in social interactions. Naturally, all the suggested activities and strategies in this book should be considered in light of your own training and the developmental levels, strengths and learning differences of the children you work with. (See Chapter 12, 'Adapting Activities', in the accompanying eBook *Using Imagination, Mindful Play and Creative Thinking to Support Wellbeing and Resilience in Children*.)

There are many different non-competitive 'mini' games that can be used for choosing groups, coordinators (leaders) and order of play where appropriate. I have listed several options in *Using Imagination, Mindful Play and Creative Thinking to Support Wellbeing and Resilience in Children* (see Chapter 14, 'Group Structures for Playing IMPACT Games'). I suggest that the format is varied between sessions so that children can experiment with different ways of doing this. The choosing then becomes part of the social and personal learning.

Reflection and discussion

Another important aspect of all the games and activities is the opportunity they provide for children to expand their thinking skills. To aid this process, I have included suggestions for further reflection and discussion ('Talk about'). These consist of a mixture of possible prompt questions as well as suggestions for comments or explanations that can be useful when introducing or elaborating some of the ideas. (For more ideas about facilitating IMPACT discussions with children, see Chapter 11, 'Mindful Communication', and Chapter 13, 'Mindful Praise and Appreciation', in *Using Imagination, Mindful Play and Creative Thinking to Support Wellbeing and Resilience in Children*.) You may want to select just a couple of these or spread the discussion over several sessions.

Discussion topics also provide an opportunity for drawing links between different themes at later times. You could remind children of particular games when this is relevant.

During all discussions it is helpful to use language that reflects the assumption that children are already doing something (however small) that will help them to manage friendships.

Expansion activities

Most of the games in this book are followed by one or more expansion activities and/or are directly linked with a second game (which could be used in the same session or later). These expansion activities and linked games are an important part of the process. They encourage children to recognize the benefits of a stepped approach to learning and to the process of change, and to understand how new skills can build on previous experiences, and how current skills can be strengthened.

Activity sheets

Some of the expansion activities have accompanying activity sheets (see section VII). These are marked with icons representing imagination and creative thinking. Of course, creative thinking and imagination are interrelated. This in itself can be a useful discussion point with children.

I have found that children particularly like to draw or write about their imaginary world. Their drawings and jottings might then be the starting point for wellbeing stories. (For ideas about how to create wellbeing stories see Chapter 17, 'Image-Making and Wellbeing Stories', and Chapter 18, 'Helping Children to Create Their Own Wellbeing Stories', in *Using Imagination, Mindful Play and Creative Thinking to Support Wellbeing and Resilience in Children*.) These can also be made into a personal 'Book of Wisdom' and perhaps act as reminders of some of the strategies that children might want to use again in the future.

Please keep in mind that IMPACT activity sheets are offered as supplementary material to expand and reinforce each child's learning experiences. They are not intended as stand-alone alternatives to the mindful play and supportive discussions that are central to the IMPACT approach.

Exploring Concepts of Friendship and Community

A MINDFUL PLAY PERSPECTIVE

Helping children to negotiate, reaffirm and build on friendship and community connections will always be relevant and worthwhile, but it is perhaps even more so in current times. The COVID-19 pandemic has once again highlighted the importance of such connections. In their *Good Childhood Report 2021*, The Children's Society, for example, suggests that while the majority of children who completed a questionnaire about wellbeing seem to have coped well with specific changes to their daily life, their responses also suggest that 'they coped less well with not being able to see friends and family, and not being able to do hobbies/pastimes'.[1]

Researchers and theorists have given us plenty of evidence to suggest that friendships are one of the important factors contributing to childhood wellbeing. And, of course, it is not just about the number of friends or social contacts that a child engages with; it is the quality of these friendships that matters. Even the experience of having one close friend can have a long-lasting influence on how a child elaborates their self-concept, how they build their self-esteem and how they develop an understanding of mutuality, empathy, loyalty and trust in relationships.

---

1   The Children's Society (2021) *The Good Childhood Report 2021: Summary*, p.14. Available at: www.childrenssociety.org.uk/information/professionals/resources/good-childhood-report-2021

IMPACT FOUNDATION ELEMENTS FOR HELPING CHILDREN TO MANAGE FRIENDSHIPS

The IMPACT approach gives emphasis to eight foundation elements for wellbeing (see Chapter 4, 'The Foundation Elements for Wellbeing', in the accompanying eBook *Using Imagination, Mindful Play and Creative Thinking to Support Wellbeing and Resilience in Children*). Since these elements are closely interconnected, changes in one will affect each of the other seven. However, the main focus for the games and activities in this book centres on three that are particularly relevant when thinking about helping children to manage friendships and to understand concepts related to community wellbeing: *self and others*, *self-awareness* and *self-reliance*.

Self and others

This foundation element involves key concepts such as empathy, compassion, respect, tolerance, trust, emotional intelligence and cooperation.

IMPACT activities explore aspects of group cooperation and trust and aim to promote an understanding of how our thoughts and actions affect our relationships with other people. They aim to help children to identify with appropriate role models and to encourage the ability to work with or alongside other children and adults with awareness and empathy.

Self-awareness

Constructive self-awareness is the cornerstone of realistic self-evaluation and can greatly enhance wellbeing. However, there are certain times in the lives of children when extra support might be needed so that an increase in self-awareness does not lead to unwanted repercussions. For example, at around the age of seven, children begin to compare themselves more directly with their peers. A child who has healthy self-esteem and age-appropriate social skills will usually weather this period well, striking a healthy balance between forming friendship groups and learning to be self-reliant.

When children do not have this solid foundation, an increase in self-awareness may lead to feelings of being 'judged' by others. This can be particularly noticeable with some children who have a communication or learning difference. Whereas they may have appeared to cope well during their early years, it is at this point that they may begin to withdraw from social contact or from participation in group activities. Social anxiety and negative expectations of how others will view them is also likely to have a direct influence on how children communicate when they do engage in interactions, resulting in further misunderstandings, embarrassment and confirmation of their difficulties.

The period of transition to secondary school is another common point at which children may experience heightened social anxiety and awareness of moments of social ineptness. Popularity with peers becomes an increasingly important issue for this age group at a time when they are also trying to cope with the challenges of larger groups and of taking more responsibility for themselves and for their learning. A child who already has difficulties with understanding and using appropriate social skills will undoubtedly find this transition period even more confusing and overwhelming. This could result in withdrawal or in the development of inappropriate behaviour in an attempt to gain recognition from peers.

The IMPACT approach offers a way of strengthening the positive aspects of self-awareness. It encourages a forum in which feelings are acknowledged, valued and openly discussed in a non-judgemental way. The games and activities help children to develop the ability to switch attention effectively between internal and external stimuli, cope more effectively with distractions, make informed choices about how and where to focus their attention, and to monitor their internal 'self-talk'. This will then help them to build skills for self-reliance.

Self-reliance

This involves developing physical, mental and emotional self-care skills, building a measure of independence and self-motivation, reducing reliance on other people's opinions and evaluations, expanding awareness of current strengths, developing the ability to realistically assess personal progress, and learning to set realistic yet challenging goals or accept the need to modify a goal.

The IMPACT approach provides opportunities for supporting children in building self-reliance by actively promoting feelings of being in control, and by helping children in their growing abilities to anticipate and predict what might happen next, both as a consequence of their own behaviour and also as a consequence of other people's behaviour. IMPACT strategies and activities also encourage and support children in the formulation of realistic and manageable goals.

Imaginative and mindful play offers a means by which we can help children to form and sustain mutually enriching friendships and connections with their wider community – connections that not only strengthen individual wellbeing and help children to build the resources for emotional resilience, but that also strengthen community wellbeing and resilience.

To get a feel for some of the activities in this book and how these relate to a child's experiences of friendships, it is helpful to start from our own perspectives. How do we, as adults, benefit and contribute to friendships and community in our own lives? Is this different to the ways in which children view their friendships? How do we already support the children in our care as they negotiate difficulties with friendships? How can we maximize this support?

Experiencing the following activities from an adult perspective will undoubtedly trigger some thoughts about how you can adapt these and other activities in this book. There are no right or wrong answers to any of these; they are simply ways of exploring the topic.

Begin by setting aside a short period of uninterrupted time when you will have the opportunity to carry out and to reflect on a single activity – 10–15 minutes is probably ample. I suggest that you only do one activity and then go back to doing other things. Please don't be tempted to do all the activities one after the other in a single sitting, even if you have the time. A period of reflection is always useful after an exploratory activity.

Exploratory activity 1.1. Me, my friendships and my community
Make a large circle from ribbon or string and lay it on the floor or on a table, leaving plenty of space around the outside of the circle to add extra rings.

Imagine that this first circle represents a group of your family and/or friends. Who, if anyone, would you place at the centre of the circle? Where would the other people be in relation to each other and in relation to the centre? Where would you place yourself at the moment? Mark the different positions with pieces of card showing other people's names or their relationship to you (friend, partner, sister, for example) or with different colours, shapes or sketches, buttons or other objects so that you are able to move them around easily.

Now think about people you know in your local community. Your contact with these people might be brief but regular, or you might know them quite well. Add these people to your first circle or around the outside of the circle in whatever space feels 'right' for you. If you have placed anyone outside your first circle, add a large concentric ring, or a separate 'satellite' ring, around these people.

Think of people you have known in the past who have been an important influence in your life. Where would you put these people? You might want to add them to a third ring that surrounds your first two rings, or place them in an existing ring.

Now think of five or more people who have some influence on your life but who you may not actually know – for example, your local councillor or the person who maintains the local park where you enjoy walking (and who might thereby contribute to your wellbeing). Where would you place these people?

Take some time to reflect on the circle(s) you have made. Notice the positioning of people and their relationship to each other. Remember: this is just a reflection of your thoughts at this moment in time and everything in your collage of circles is moveable.

So now, in the spirit of play, are there any adjustments that you would like to make to the future positioning of people in relation to yourself? If so, how might you rearrange your collage?

How would it feel to remove the rings from your collage? What would that signify to you? You may or may not want to physically remove the rings to see what that is like. Again, there is no right or wrong configuration – this is just an exploration.

And finally, if you have made any adjustments, ask yourself, 'What am I already doing that will help this change to happen?' and 'What would be the smallest *next* step that would help this change to happen?'

Adaptation for children

This activity is easily adapted for children. One example of how this might be done is given in '10. Friendships and community' in section III.

Exploratory activity 1.2. Finding an image of friendship

(This is based on ImageWork exercises by Dr Dina Glouberman.[2])

In order to avoid distractions, this activity will be maximally effective if you read through the guidance a couple of times and then carry out the activity with your eyes closed. I suggest that you also have some paper and pencils

---

2   See, for example, Glouberman, D. (2003) *Life Choices, Life Changes*. London: Hodder & Stoughton; Glouberman, D. (2014) *You Are What You Imagine*. London: Watkins Publishing.; Glouberman, D. (2022) *ImageWork*. Monmouth: PCCS Books.

close to hand. For guidance on using imagery please see the accompanying eBook *Using Imagination, Mindful Play and Creative Thinking to Support Wellbeing and Resilience in Children*, in particular Chapter 8, 'Imagination and Images', and Chapter 9, 'Image-Making'.

When you are ready, settle yourself in a comfortable position and allow your eyes to close. Breathe slowly and fully three times – in through your nose and out through your mouth. Then forget about your breathing. As your mind and body start to relax, allow an image to emerge that somehow represents the best part of what it means to be a friend. This image could be an animal, a person, an object, a plant or bird or a colour. Just let an image appear in your mind and go with whatever comes for you.

When you have an image, allow yourself plenty of time to explore it as fully as possible. What does it look like, sound like, feel like? If it can move, how does it move? Explore your image from above and below and all the way round it.

Now imagine that you can become this image. Step into being this image. Take a full breath and breathe out slowly. Feel how it is to be this image of friendship. How do you feel physically, mentally, emotionally?

When you feel that you have a sense of what it's like to be this image, ask yourself the following questions – again, give yourself plenty of time to explore each one:

- What is the best thing about being you (the image)?
- What are the important qualities of this image?
- As this image, what are your best hopes? What do you most need? What would you like to happen next?

You may find it useful to have a conversation with the image. Swap back and forth between being the image and being 'self' so that you can find out more about what this image means to you and how it represents the best part of what it means to be a friend.

When you are ready, finish as 'self' and allow the image to fade.

Sit quietly for a few moments and think about what the image meant for you, and how this relates to your friendships. When you are ready, open your eyes and draw or write about your image.

THE CREATIVE SUBCONSCIOUS

Working with images can often precipitate shifts in perception or awaken new ideas. This can be helpful for children too, and can be a fun and often transformative way of exploring ideas and feelings. Neurofeedback research appears to add emphasis to what we already know. Helping children to develop, recognize and value their abilities to focus, relax and imagine can be beneficial to their wellbeing and can have repercussions for their social connections. If they are able to continue to develop and value these capacities, this may affect their wellbeing in the long term too.

> **Neuro nugget**
>
> Different brain wave rhythms reflect different states of consciousness. For example, alpha rhythms indicate a relaxed state while theta brain waves are low frequency waves that have been associated with the creative subconscious mind. Dr Shanida Nataraja describes how neurofeedback – where brain wave patterns are translated into images on a screen – has been used to help people to train themselves to recognize different rhythms and to switch from one rhythm to another. Dr Nataraja notes that 'alpha/theta feedback has been reported to improve artistry in musical students and dance performance in ballroom and Latin dance champions', and that such feedback has also been associated with people being 'more compassionate, emotionally stable, socially bold, relaxed and satisfied', perhaps because of changes in mood.[3]

FRIENDSHIPS AND COMMUNITY

Exploratory activity 1.3. Community wellbeing

For this activity, instead of drawing something at the end of an imagery exercise, start by sitting with paper and pencils and draw whatever image comes to mind that somehow represents 'community wellbeing'. Don't think about this beforehand or plan what to draw – just allow a free flow of

---

3   Nataraja, S. (2008) *The Blissful Brain*. London: Gaia, Octopus Publishing Group Ltd.

your imagination. If you are usually right-handed, try drawing with your left hand, and vice versa.

When you feel that you have finished, add something surprising.

Take some time to think about your drawing or put it where you can easily see it at various times during the day. Allow your mind to elaborate on your image of community wellbeing and perhaps note what image represents your opposite of this.

In other books in this series I have shared images that emerged as I was writing. These images have all been the result of very brief explorations (no more than a couple of minutes) and illustrate how images can sum up a personal perspective very easily and naturally. So, this is my image of 'community wellbeing':

The image that emerges for me is one of a 'spider blanket'. I realize that this has been triggered by seeing a picture of a spider blanket in the news a while ago. Some spiders apparently join together to make a strong blanket of webs to help them to cope with flooding.

As a spider blanket, I feel strong, beautiful and special. My best hope is that my strength (as a blanket) will help me through rough times. What I most need is plenty of spiders who are willing to join to help me (the blanket) work well.

When I imagine being one of the spiders I feel more vulnerable but I see myself as persistent – when my single web breaks I repair it or build another one, making more, and stronger, connections with other spiders and their webs. The whole blanket nourishes me and houses me, and it also nourishes and houses the community of spiders.

This is a fairly obvious metaphor for mutuality in friendships and communities but, of course, some people would have a different response to spiders, perhaps remembering various films in which spiders are less than friendly! The important point is that we will each have different images for similar concepts and that our images may change over time.

EXPLORING EMPATHY

There are some recognizable and widely accepted aspects of friendships that are almost a 'given' if that friendship is to be mutually enriching and supportive. One of these is the development of empathy. Empathy is a term freely used but sometimes misunderstood. In counselling relationships it has a very specific meaning. Carl Rogers' definition highlights the profound and powerful nature of an empathic relationship:

> It means entering the private perceptual world of the other and becoming thoroughly at home in it. It involves being sensitive, moment by moment, to the changing felt meanings which flow in this other person... It means temporarily living the other's life, moving about in it delicately without making judgements... It means frequently checking with the person as to the accuracy of your sensing, and being guided by the responses you receive.[4]

Embryonic signs of empathy can be seen in young children, such as when they try to comfort a distressed peer (although such comforting may sometimes be in response to their own feeling of unease and distress). Helping older children to understand that they can be empathic without experiencing the same event or circumstance that a friend is dealing with can also help them to offer emotional support in friendships without being overwhelmed by the other person's feelings.

Exploratory activity 1.4. Associative sensitivity

Think of a time when you have felt that a friend, colleague or family member has truly understood your feelings about an event or circumstance. What aspects of your interaction led to this understanding? What did you both do and say?

Think of a time when you felt that you have suddenly 'got it' when talking with a child. What aspects of your interaction led to this understanding? What were you thinking/doing/saying? If you could come up with an image that somehow represented how that child was feeling, what would that image be?

Sometimes we can be so empathically in tune with someone else that we might have a

---

4   Rogers (1980), quoted in Hargarden, H. and Sills, C. (2002) *Transactional Analysis: A Relational Perspective.* Hove and New York: Brunner-Routledge.

spontaneous image that reflects how they are feeling. In a therapeutic context Murray Cox and Alice Theilgaard refer to this level of attunement as a form of 'associative sensitivity'.[5] Although working in the field of psychotherapy and medical psychology, their exploration of this phenomenon is relevant to our everyday encounters too. It is worth bearing this in mind and perhaps noting moments of associative sensitivity during some of the 'Talk about' sections in the games and activities in this book. Occasionally sharing an image ('From what you are all telling me, I have this image of a storm cloud floating round the room') gives you the opportunity to help children to extend their imaginative capabilities and demonstrates a way that children can also share images to help explain and understand their feelings (see 'Offering an image' in Chapter 9, 'Image-Making', in the accompanying eBook *Using Imagination, Mindful Play and Creative Thinking to Support Wellbeing and Resilience in Children*).

In summary, the IMPACT approach to managing friendships encourages children to engage in imaginative and mindful play as a way to enhance their understanding of the complexities and joys of friendships and of community with others, recognize their current strengths, build new skills and have fun while learning.

---

5   Cox, M. and Theilgaard, A. (1997) *Mutative Metaphors in Psychotherapy: The Aeolian Mode*. London: Jessica Kingsley Publishers.

IMPACT Essentials for Managing Friendships

By doing the activities in this section you will be helping children to:

- think about different aspects of themselves, not just how they are dealing with any current difficulties
- identify their resources, strengths and skills
- see themselves as active participants in change
- begin to explore how the ability to imagine can be a helpful resource
- continue to develop or consolidate their skills in focusing and attending.

1. What's my name?

Wellbeing focus:

☑ Self and others   ☑ Self-reliance

☑ Self-awareness

Examples of personal skills learned or consolidated:

☑ Listening   ☑ Taking turns

☑ Asking questions   ☑ Concentration

Examples of general/social learning:

☑ Being part of a group   ☑ Building group cohesion

☑ Development of body awareness   ☑ Building trust
  and positive body image

This is a useful introductory game, particularly for a new group, but it could also be played in a group where everyone already knows each other. The emphasis is on self-respect and respect for others. It is also an opportunity to begin discussions about existing skills and how these might help when looking at new challenges. For more ideas about identifying and utilizing current skills, see Chapter 5, 'Making Experience Count', in the accompanying eBook *Using Imagination, Mindful Play and Creative Thinking to Support Wellbeing and Resilience in Children*.

(See also '3. Skills and brills' and '8. Getting to know you'.)

How to play

Players write their name (or how they would like to be known) on a sticky label. They hide the label somewhere on their own clothes, in the top of their sock, in a pocket, under their collar or on the sole of their shoe, for example.

Without touching anyone, players try to find as many names as possible (within a time limit suitable for the size of the group). They can only ask questions such as 'Is it on the sole of your shoe?' or 'Can you show me underneath your right foot?' They either write down all the names that they find or try to remember them.

When the time limit is up everyone stands or sits in a circle. The game coordinator stands behind each person in turn and everyone tries to remember that person's name.

Adaptations

- Instead of their names, players write one of their skills or something that they enjoy doing. Players need to find the sticker and at the same time find out each person's name.
- Players write positive descriptions of themselves, such as 'cool' or 'friendly'.

Talk about

Do you have a favourite name? How do you like to be known?

Why are names important? What helps you to remember other people's names? What might make it easier? What might make it harder? What feelings do you have when other people remember your name?

What skills did you use for this game? Can you think of a time when you have used these skills before? How might these skills be helpful in this group/at school/at home?

EXPANSION ACTIVITY 1.1. THE STORIES WE TELL (1)

Invite the children to research and then share the story of their name, for example what they know of its origin and how it was chosen. This could be done in pairs or in the whole group if time allows. (For a longer version of this game, see '7. Story-line' in *Helping Children to Build Self-Confidence*, which is also available in this series.) Children write about or draw the story of their name (see 'Activity sheet 1.1. My name story').

2. Parachute name game

Wellbeing focus:

☑ Self and others   ☑ Self-reliance
☑ Self-awareness

Examples of personal skills learned or consolidated:

☑ Listening   ☑ Concentration
☑ Taking turns

Examples of general/social learning:

☑ Being part of a group   ☑ Understanding how and why
☑ Development of body awareness   rules are made
   and positive body image   ☑ Understanding how individual
☑ Building group cohesion   behaviour affects others
☑ Building trust

Note: As with all games involving the use of equipment, parachute games need to be supervised by an adult. This 'rule' can be a useful prompt for a discussion about why some rules are needed for safety reasons (see 'Talk about' below). See also '21. Waves on the sea parachute game' in Helping Children to Manage Anger, another title in this series.

How to play
Players crouch down around the outside of the parachute, holding tightly to the edge. On a signal from the game coordinator (or the children take turns to say 'One, two, three, up') everyone jumps up, making the parachute mushroom into the air. The coordinator quickly calls the names of two players who try to swap places by running underneath the parachute before it floats back down.

Adaptation

• Players hold the parachute at waist level. A large soft ball is placed in the middle of the parachute. The coordinator says the name of each player in turn, and everyone tries to send the ball across the circle to that person.

Talk about

What are the rules for this game? Do all games have rules? Why do you think this? What are some of the rules that help to make a game feel safe?

Sometimes rules are 'unspoken'. How do you find out about the different rules for different groups?

What rules shall we have for this group?

Are there any 'rules' that help us to make and to develop friendships? Do you think there are any 'safety' rules for friendships?

Can you think of some rules that might be useful for communities? What about rules for our natural environment? For example, are there any safety rules about walking or cycling in the country or in parks that relate to care of wildlife? Are there any safety rules about litter that relate to wildlife? Who makes these rules?

Can you think of another word for 'rules'? Is there a difference between rules, laws, suggestions and guidelines? If so, how do they differ?

If you had the chance to make up a new rule, suggestion or guideline for your class/school/friendship group/community, what would it be? How easy or difficult do you think it would be to get everyone involved in following this?

EXPANSION ACTIVITY 2.1. WISDOM RULES!

Suggest to the children that they write a list of rules for the group and/or their community. Use this to start (or add to) their personal 'Book of Wisdom' or start a shared 'Book of Wisdom' for the whole group (see activity sheet 2.1).

EXPANSION ACTIVITY 2.2. CONFLICT RESOLUTION

'Parachute name game' could be revisited at a later stage and the discussion extended to include exploration of conflict resolution skills and some of the preferred 'guidelines' for this type of interaction (see the notes for 'Activities' in section I).

3. Skills and brills

Wellbeing focus:

☑ Self and others   ☑ Self-reliance
☑ Self-awareness

Examples of personal skills learned or consolidated:

☑ Organizing   ☑ Speaking in a group
☑ Sharing personal information

Examples of general/social learning:

☑ Building self-respect and respect   ☑ Exploring self-efficacy
  for others   ☑ Building trust

(See also '1. What's my name?')

Building on a child's current strengths and skills is an important aspect of the IMPACT approach and features in other games throughout this series of books (see, for example, 'Expansion activity 4.1. Skills wheel' in *Helping Children to Manage Anger*).

How to play

Ask the children to each think of something that they love to do and what skills they have that help them to love doing this. They then draw or write about each of their skills on separate pieces of coloured paper. If you are working with a group, I suggest that you start with an upper limit of five skills each to avoid competition between players.

Pin the pieces of paper to individual cloaks (large squares of material) for the children to wear.

Volunteers talk about their skills cloak to the rest of the group. (There is a suggested format for building confidence in talking in front of groups in Chapter 13, 'Mindful Praise and Appreciation', in the accompanying eBook *Using Imagination, Mindful Play and Creative Thinking to Support Wellbeing and Resilience in Children*. There is also an elaborated version of this in the session outlines that can be found in *Helping Children to Build Self-Confidence*, another title in this series.)

Adaptations

- This also works well as a collaborative activity. In this instance the children could make a single large cloak or wall hanging together. This could be used to explore the many ways that different children might utilize their skills and strengths to tackle the same challenges. It is also a very positive way to look at individual strengths at the start of a new group and to explore how these will contribute to the ways in which the group will function effectively.

- Use one or more of the drawing templates available in Appendix C of the accompanying eBook *Using Imagination, Mindful Play and Creative Thinking to Support Wellbeing and Resilience in Children* for children to draw themselves wearing their skills cloak, or to write about themselves, noting personal qualities and skills that they would like other people to know about. Add this to their 'Book of Wisdom'. Encourage the children to imagine putting on their skills cloak when they are about to undertake a new task.

Talk about

How can these skills help us in other ways? (For example, a child might identify observation skills, patience or knowing how to make and use a 'hide' as things that help them to enjoy wildlife photography. These can then be 'mapped' on to other situations such as having the patience to persevere with a task, being able to control their focus of attention and being able to stay calm in a difficult situation.)

Everyone has valuable skills. What skill are you most proud of? What are you already brilliant at? What is the difference between boasting and being proud about something?

We can always add more skills to our skills cloaks. What will be different when your skills cloak has even more 'friendship' skills? How will your teacher/ friends/brother/sister know that you are wearing your (imaginary) skills cloak?

What would you most like to achieve in this group? What skills do you already have that will help you to achieve this?

EXPANSION ACTIVITY 3.1. LUCKY DIP

Each child chooses one of the skills from their cloak and places this piece of paper in a bowl or hat. They each then take a lucky dip and see what skill they come up with. Perhaps it is a skill that they haven't got on their own cloak, but would like to have. Can they guess who is the owner of this skill? The children then talk about how they might use this new skill, or, if it is already one that they have on their own cloak, do they perhaps use the skill in a different way? This might also highlight skills that the children may have forgotten to put on their own cloaks or hadn't thought about. Finish by returning each skill to its owner to be pinned onto their cloak again.

4. The moon is round

Wellbeing focus:

- ☑ Self and others
- ☑ Self-awareness

- ☑ Self-reliance

Examples of personal skills learned or consolidated:

- ☑ Focusing and shifting attention
- ☑ Observation
- ☑ Listening

- ☑ Memory strategies
- ☑ Tolerating frustration
- ☑ Problem-solving

Examples of general/social learning:

- ☑ Reducing impulsivity and building persistence

- ☑ Understanding different perspectives

This is a fun game for helping children to understand the skill of focusing and shifting attention. The next game, '5. Sleeping bear', offers an opportunity for discussion about the links between focusing attention and concentrating for longer periods. (See also Chapter 7, 'Helping Children to Be Mindful', in the accompanying eBook *Using Imagination, Mindful Play and Creative Thinking to Support Wellbeing and Resilience in Children*.)

How to play

Players sit in a circle. The game coordinator introduces the activity by saying, 'See if you can do exactly as I do.' They then 'draw' a circle, two dots and two lines in the air in front of them. As they draw, they say: 'The moon is round, it has two eyes, a nose and a mouth.' When they have finished drawing the moon they fold their arms. They then ask for a volunteer from the group to have a go. Players are usually so focused on the drawing of the moon that they don't notice that the sequence must be completed by folding their arms. The coordinator may eventually need to make the arm folding more obvious so that all the children can guess the 'trick'.

Adaptations

- Involve one of the players as a coordinator by explaining the trick to them secretly before the group gets together.
- The game coordinator draws the moon on the floor using a stick in their right hand. When they have finished drawing, they put the stick in the centre of the circle of players using their left hand. Players need to do the same to make their floor drawing.
- The game coordinator uses a bunch of keys or five sticks/pencils to show players 'a riddle about counting'. They shake the keys in their closed hands and throw them gently on the floor. They then lean forward and look at the keys closely, at the same time placing three fingertips on the floor. After looking at the keys carefully they say 'That's a three'. They do this twice more with a different number of fingers each time, for example 'That's a ten', 'That's a zero'. Now see if players can guess how the coordinator is counting.

Talk about

What did you feel when you were trying to work out the trick? What did you feel when you suddenly 'got it'? Can you think of any other times when you have been puzzled by something and then suddenly understood it? What helps you to work things out in this way?

In this game you focused your attention on one thing and then shifted it to something else. Can you think of other times when this might be a useful skill?

How might focusing and listening skills be helpful in our friendships?

EXPANSION ACTIVITY 4.1. GREEN SPACE MOON FOCUS

Start by doing some brief research about the phases of the moon as a group. Collect objects from nature to make into a circular collage depicting the cycle from new moon to full moon and back to new moon. Lay the collage out in a large open space. Talk about the time that it takes for the moon to go through a full cycle. Walk slowly around the large circle in pairs or threes, breathing mindfully together (see 'Mindful breathing' in Appendix A in the accompanying eBook *Using Imagination, Mindful Play and Creative Thinking to Support Wellbeing and Resilience in Children*). Finish with everyone sitting around the outside of the circle.

Talk about
(See also section III.)

How did you feel when you were walking around the circle together?

Think about the ways in which groups sometimes go through 'phases' – starting, growing together, completing a task together, and coming to a close. Think about what is helpful and what is difficult about working in a group.

What are some of the helpful and difficult aspects about gradual change and sudden change?

In this activity you worked together to make the collage. Was that easy or difficult? Why was that? In the first game ('4. The moon is round') you tried to work out the 'trick' on your own. Did anyone help you out? How did that feel?

5. Sleeping bear

Wellbeing focus:

- ☑ Self and others
- ☑ Self-awareness
- ☑ Self-reliance

Examples of personal skills learned or consolidated:

- ☑ Listening
- ☑ Tolerating frustration
- ☑ Self-control
- ☑ Problem-solving

Examples of general/social learning:

- ☑ Development of body awareness and positive body image
- ☑ Recognizing that learning can span several subjects at the same time

How to play

The game coordinator chooses the first person to be the bear. This person sits on a chair in the middle of the circle or at the far end of the room, blind-folded. A bunch of keys is placed under the chair. The game coordinator chooses a player to creep up to the chair and grab the keys before the bear can point at them. If they manage to get the keys, they become the new bear.

Adaptations

- Put newspaper or crumpled brown paper on the floor to make it extra difficult to move quietly.
- Two players at a time cross the room from opposite ends. They imagine that it is night-time and both keep their eyes shut. One is a wildlife photographer and one is the bear. They must both move slowly and cautiously and listen carefully. The photographer tries to find and point to the bear and the bear tries to stay away from the photographer.
- Shorten or lengthen the starting distance between the bear and the photographer.

Talk about

In this game players focused their attention on listening and on moving carefully and quietly. How easy or difficult is it for you to move in this way? What skills did you need?

How easy or difficult is it for you to hear someone moving when you have your eyes closed?

What skills did you use when you were the bear? What skills did the photographer use?

What is the difference between hearing and listening? How can listening and looking skills help us in our friendships?

EXPANSION ACTIVITY 5.1. IN FOCUS

Children research the skills that are needed for night-time photography and identify one skill that they already have. This could then lead to discussions and exploration of the innovative ways in which night-time photography can be used (for example, painting with light) and how skills for one activity can be extended and enhanced or used for something completely different.

6. Imagination tent

Wellbeing focus:

☑ Self and others   ☑ Self-reliance
☑ Self-awareness

Examples of personal skills learned or consolidated:

☑ Focusing attention   ☑ Taking turns
☑ Self-calming   ☑ Time-keeping

Examples of general/social learning:

☑ Developing dramatic awareness   ☑ Flexibility of thought

This game also links with '36. Inner expert'. (For guidance on using imagery with children, see Chapter 8, 'Imagination and Images', and Chapter 9, 'Image-Making', in the accompanying eBook *Using Imagination, Mindful Play and Creative Thinking to Support Wellbeing and Resilience in Children*.)

An imagination tent has so many potential uses that you might find that you want to build a larger semi-permanent structure in one corner of a room or outside in a sheltered spot. In this game the tent is used for focus activities.

How to play

Make a tent by draping a small parachute or a large piece of cloth over a table-top (see the 'Talk about' section for '2. Parachute name game'). This is now an imagination tent. Perhaps the children can invent a special name for this place, such as 'The Imagination Emporium' or 'The Image-Making Magicians' Palace'! Each time this special place is visited it becomes a different environment where the imagination is celebrated. For example:

- Players imagine that they are going into a spaceship and when they land (that is, come out from under the table) they will be in a different world. What can they see? What can they hear?
- Players lie under the table with their feet towards the centre and their heads outside the parachute 'tent'. With eyes closed, they imagine that it

is night-time and they are all on a camping trip in an unusual or previously unexplored location. What can they hear? What can they smell? What might the ground feel like?

- Players imagine that they are going into a time machine. They can go forwards or back in time. They all negotiate a chosen time to travel to. When they come out of the time machine what do they see? What can they hear?

Adaptations

- If you only have room for one small table to be prepared in this way, the children could line up and go through the tent one at a time. This is a good opportunity for one of the children to take on the role of game coordinator. They stand at the entrance and 'welcome' each player to the tent. A second coordinator or timekeeper could hold the cloth on the opposite side of the tent to allow the children to crawl out, saying goodbye to them.
- Children who do not enjoy small spaces might be more comfortable passing through a curtain or going behind a room divider.

Talk about

In this game you used your imagination. What is the best thing about being able to imagine something that isn't really happening?

How can the ability to imagine help friends and group members to get on with each other?

How could you use the imagination tent for other games? Can you 'invent' an imagination listening game that we all could play?

Being Part of a Group

By doing the activities in this section you will be helping children to:

- understand the importance of self-respect and respect for others
- think about the differences between being part of a group and working or playing independently
- understand that friendship groups can be very fluid in structure
- explore the concept of peer pressure
- think about some of the ways in which individual skills and personal qualities can contribute to group and community wellbeing.

7. Party guests

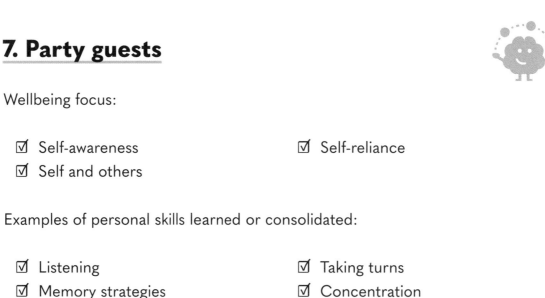

Wellbeing focus:

- ☑ Self-awareness
- ☑ Self and others
- ☑ Self-reliance

Examples of personal skills learned or consolidated:

- ☑ Listening
- ☑ Memory strategies
- ☑ Taking turns
- ☑ Concentration

Examples of general/social learning:

- ☑ Developing sensitivity to other people's strengths and challenges
- ☑ Understanding different perspectives
- ☑ Building self-respect and respect for others

This game links with '8. Getting to know you'.

How to play

Each player thinks of a fact that they would like other group members to know about them. Aim for this to be a personal statement about an ability, like or dislike. Players introduce themselves to each other in pairs and share their personal statements. All pairs then walk around the room together introducing their partners and responding to introductions from others. For example, 'This is Moira and she loves swimming', 'Hello Moira, I'm Jan and this is Ryan. He's really good at drawing cartoons.'

Adaptations

- As a group, think about a limited number of possible facts that players can then choose from.
- Players invent something amazing to say about their partner based on what is already known about their interests and personality. For example, 'This is Moira and she is the youngest person ever to swim the Channel.'

Talk about

Did you find anyone who has the same talent or like/dislike as you?

How do you feel when you hear someone introduce you in this way?

How do we show that we appreciate and respect our own and other people's talents and abilities?

Children don't normally introduce each other in such a formal way, but when might such formal introductions be used? How else might we get to know more about each other?

8. Getting to know you

Wellbeing focus:

- ☑ Self and others
- ☑ Self-awareness
- ☑ Self-reliance

Examples of personal skills learned or consolidated:

- ☑ Listening
- ☑ Memory strategies
- ☑ Taking turns
- ☑ Concentration

Examples of general/social learning:

- ☑ Appreciating diversity
- ☑ Building self-respect and respect for others

This activity can be used as an expansion activity for '7. Party guests'. As with '1. What's my name?', it can also be a fun activity for children who already know each other.

How to play

Players split into teams and secretly devise their own list of five statements to ask another team. They can use activity sheet 8 as a starting point for some ideas. Each team tries to think of four statements that might be true for most members of another team and one statement that might be unique to a member of their own team.

Adaptation

- Each player uses activity sheet 8 as a prompt for questioning the rest of the group or to write down the names of anyone they find who agrees with the statements.

Talk about

Did you find lots of similarities between group members or lots of differences?

Did you find out anything about someone that you didn't already know? Did anything surprise you?

How do you feel when you know that you have things in common with other people? Was it difficult or easy to find things in common? Was it difficult or easy to find something that is unique to just one person?

Why is it helpful to try and remember what people tell us about themselves? What would make it easier/harder to remember important information about other people? What does it feel like when someone remembers something important about you? What does it feel like when people forget what you have told them, or if they get the facts mixed up?

What does this game tell us about respecting ourselves and respecting others?

EXPANSION ACTIVITY 8.1. DESCRIBING PEOPLE

Using activity sheets 8.1a and 8.1b, as a group, think about words and phrases that can be used to describe people in a positive way. Ask the children to imagine how they might feel if they heard someone describing them in this way. Remind the children about what is acceptable.

(The children complete one or both activity sheets as appropriate for the group.)

Talk about

People are unlikely to change most physical features from one day to the next but could, for example, change their hair colour or have their ears pierced. In contrast, how we act and how we feel can change from moment to moment. For example, feelings can change from the start of a group to the end of a group. Someone who is thoughtful might sometimes do something that is not thoughtful, but that doesn't mean that they are no longer a thoughtful person. What do you think are some of the different feelings that some children might have about being in a group? Do you think some adults might have the same or different feelings?

Can you think of ways in which your actions or thoughts have changed since the beginning of term/in the last month/since your last birthday? Have any of these changes happened because of being with a group of friends, or because of other people's actions or what they have said to you? Have any of these changes happened because you made a decision to change? Did any happen without you realizing at the time?

Is there something that you like to do or dislike doing that you think will always be the same for you?

9. Five and a joker

Wellbeing focus:

- ☑ Self and others
- ☑ Self-awareness
- ☑ Self-reliance

Examples of personal skills learned or consolidated:

- ☑ Observation
- ☑ Memory strategies
- ☑ Concentration
- ☑ Asking questions

Examples of general/social learning:

- ☑ Awareness of others
- ☑ Awareness of the wider environment
- ☑ Building self-respect and respect for others
- ☑ Appreciating diversity

How to play

Pairs of players take turns to sit in the centre of the group. They have an allotted time to study each other carefully, noting hair colour, eye colour, clothes, etc. They then turn and sit back-to-back. The rest of the group call out questions such as 'What colour are Becky's socks?' The players in the centre score one point for every correct answer. At any time during their turn a player can use a 'joker' before answering. This will give them five points if they are correct. The round continues until both players in the centre have 10 points each.

Adaptations

- The length of time allocated for observation is increased or decreased.
- The same set of questions is used for each pair.
- Three players sit in the centre and work as a team to answer questions about each other. Any one of them can use the 'joker' to help the team to gain their 10 points in the fastest time possible.

Talk about

How did you feel when you spent time looking at each other?

How could observation skills and memory strategies help us in our friendships? (For example, noticing a friend's emotions, remembering a friend's birthday, or remembering something that they like to do.)

What happened when three players worked together to remember what they had observed?

10. Friendships and community

Wellbeing focus:

☑ Self and others   ☑ Self-reliance

☑ Self-awareness

Examples of personal skills learned or consolidated:

☑ Listening   ☑ Concentration

☑ Cooperation

Examples of general/social learning:

☑ Learning the social value of   ☑ Appreciating diversity
    individual skills and abilities

How to play

(See also 'Exploratory activity 1.1. Me, my friendships and my community'.)

Begin by making a large circle from string and laying it on the floor or on a table, leaving plenty of space around the outside of the circle to add extra rings. At each stage, the children are given the choice of adding concentric rings or 'satellite' rings.

Players imagine that this first circle represents everyone who is part of the current group. Each child places their name, or a small object that somehow represents them, inside the circle.

Ask the children to think about family members. Each child adds just one object or a card to represent 'family' around the outside of the circle. They then work together to place a large circle around the 'family' section. Now they do the same for 'friends' – again, each child uses just one object or card to represent friends. They make another ring for people they know in their local community, and another ring for people they may not have met but who they know play an important role in the community (such as local hospital staff, the police, the local refuse collectors, water company staff). Now they add a ring to represent all the other people who live in each child's neighbourhood but who they think may not have any connection with them.

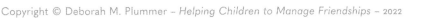

Adaptations

- Decorating a handful of pebbles and placing them in large hoops is one way in which children can have fun with this.

- Construct the collage outside with objects collected from nature to represent each grouping of people. Take photos of the collage for children to add to their 'Book of Wisdom'.

- A variation of this activity can be used to help individual children to identify their emotional resources and skills (the inner circle), and their helpers, such as family, friends, mentors and teachers (one or more outer circles). (For more about resources for resilience see Chapter 2, 'Wellbeing and Resilience', in the accompanying eBook *Using Imagination, Mindful Play and Creative Thinking to Support Wellbeing and Resilience in Children*. See also activities '9. The resilience tree' and '10. Skill mix' in *Helping Children to Manage Transitions*, another title in this series.) This can be extended to discussing and drawing important events and places. What 'gift' have these important people, places and events given to the children that will help them to manage friendships now and in the future? For example, an important place might be somewhere that they could go, or could imagine themselves being, when they need to re-energize or calm themselves. Perhaps an important person has some wise advice about managing friendships or might simply be someone who 'understands'. An important event might be a time when a friend shared a special day out.

Talk about

This activity will naturally engender discussion during the process. When the children have finished their collage of rings, ask them how they would feel if one or more rings (not the cards or objects) were removed from the collage. Does that make a difference to where any of the cards or objects are placed? How could this affect how we think about a community? Why might that be?

Are friendship groups usually very separate or could someone be part of more than one friendship group? When might this happen? Can anyone share their experience of this?

11. Community skills

Wellbeing focus:

- ☑ Self-awareness
- ☑ Self and others
- ☑ Self-reliance

Examples of personal skills learned or consolidated:

- ☑ Listening
- ☑ Cooperation
- ☑ Negotiating

Examples of general/social learning:

- ☑ Learning the social value of individual skills and achievements
- ☑ Appreciating diversity
- ☑ Understanding concept of peer pressure

This game is an adapted and extended version of '5. Skill swap', which can be found in *Helping Children to Manage Anger*, another book in this series. It requires some preparation by facilitators beforehand. There should be no element of win or lose. The main emphasis is on how the players are able to negotiate and cooperate, how sets of skills are needed for different activities, and how the same skills can be used in a variety of circumstances.

How to play

You will need to make a list of about 20 different community skills. These might be fairly obvious, such as 'Organizational skills', or take a little more thought, such as 'Skilled at listening'. The list is left on display for players to refer to throughout the game. Make a second copy on card that can be cut up into separate skills. Shuffle the cards and divide them equally between two teams of players.

Each team needs skills for community tasks that are very different to each other. For example, Team A has 'Playing football' and Team B has 'Walking a dog for someone who is housebound'. Or Team A has 'Organizing a group outing' and Team B has 'Cutting up vegetables for a community BBQ'.

The teams check through their cards and decide which skills they want to keep for their task. They then decide what they don't need.

Now they take turns to negotiate a skill swap with the other team. The children work out the best way to do this, but if they are struggling, you could suggest examples such as 'We need listening skills. We can give you skills for research'. The other team then confer but might respond with 'No, we need listening skills because ___ [they need to give a valid reason] but we can give you observation skills'. Or 'Yes, you can have listening skills, but only if you give us two of your skills'.

Each team has a maximum of five opportunities for swaps. You could also consider having some spare duplicate cards that teams could request after their five swaps.

Each team discusses the outcome among themselves and then chooses one person to give feedback to the whole group about what happened.

Adaptations

- Before starting the game, each team is asked to devise a 'rule' for swapping fairly.
- All players are given a provided list of people to find and one or more community skills cards. For example, a skill card might be 'Able to drive a large bus' and the instructions could include 'Find someone who could help groups of children get to school on time'. When they have found a suitable match, they write down the person's name or their occupation on their list.

Talk about

What happened during the trading? What worked? What didn't work?

Were the rules useful? Why was this?

Did players have a team 'strategy'? If so, did this work? If not, what strategy might have worked? (The most effective way of completing this task would be for both teams to cooperate with each other from the start. They could, for example, pool all their cards and then share them out appropriately. What would prevent this from happening? What would help this to happen?)

What skills are needed for negotiating and cooperating as a group? What do you think is one of your best skills?

This game can also engender discussion about community values, leadership, loyalties and peer pressure.

12. Find the leader

Wellbeing focus:

- ☑ Self-awareness
- ☑ Self and others

- ☑ Self-reliance

Examples of personal skills learned or consolidated:

- ☑ Problem-solving
- ☑ Understanding and using non-verbal communication

- ☑ Concentration
- ☑ Observation

Examples of general/social learning:

- ☑ Building group cohesion
- ☑ Understanding how individual behaviour affects others

- ☑ Building persistence
- ☑ Understanding the concept of peer pressure

How to play

One person (the 'detective') leaves the room while the others choose a leader. The detective returns and stands in the middle of the circle. Players in the circle have to copy everything the leader does and the detective tries to spot who the leader is.

Adaptation

- Have two leaders and two detectives. Half the players copy one leader and the other half copy the second leader (this could be done alternately round the circle, for example).

Talk about

How do leaders ensure they have the attention of the players? Does everyone watch the leader or is it sometimes a chain reaction? What does 'leading by example' mean? How is this different from leading by instruction?

As with '11. Community skills', this game could be revisited at a later time in order to expand the discussion to cover such topics as leadership qualities, loyalties and peer pressure.

13. The stories we tell (2)

Help the children to make a list of qualities and skills associated with successful friendship groups. Make up a story or puppet play together about a group of people or animals who have forgotten how to use any of these qualities or skills. What will happen when they get together to plan a holiday or to build a spaceship, for example?

For older children, there is a well-known workplace 'story' that involves an important task to complete. The four characters in this story are Somebody, Anybody, Nobody and Everybody. This could be used as a basis for children to invent their own story about responsibility, although the concepts can be difficult to grasp at first! They could perhaps think about these four characters having responsibility for a community task, such as making a community garden or clearing the school playground of litter: Somebody dropped their sweet wrappers in the playground. Nobody saw them do it. Everybody said Somebody had to pick the wrappers up, but Somebody said Anybody could have dropped them and Everybody should pick them up. Everybody disagreed...and so on!

IV

Understanding Friendships

By doing the activities in this section you will be helping children to:

- develop or consolidate their understanding of a range of different emotions and how to recognize and respond to other children's emotions, for example noticing when a friend is upset and offering to help[1]
- share and expand on personal thoughts and feelings
- continue to build or consolidate self-respect and respect for others
- build or consolidate their understanding of loyalty and trust in friendships
- further their understanding of how our thoughts and actions affect our relationships with other people.

---

1   Some psychologists make a distinction between *feelings* (such as feelings of wellbeing, thirst or pain) and *emotions* (such as anger or sadness). Since we don't tend to do this in our daily interactions, I have used the terms interchangeably in the relevant games and activities.

14. Feel it, do it

Wellbeing focus:

☑ Self and others   ☑ Self-reliance
☑ Self-awareness

Examples of personal skills learned or consolidated:

☑ Understanding feelings   ☑ Observation
☑ Taking turns   ☑ Listening

Examples of general/social learning:

☑ Understanding empathy   ☑ Developing body awareness and
                                       positive body image

(See also '15. Living pelmanism'.)

How to play

Players stand in a circle facing each other. Volunteers take turns to step into the circle and show with their whole body the way that they are feeling today. Then they say their name (in a way that also reflects the emotion) and step back. The whole group steps forward and reflects back the action and the original person's name. Everyone steps back. The next volunteer steps forward. Players do not need to name the emotions.

Adaptations

- Players start by crouching down low. Volunteers jump up and then crouch down again when they have shown their feeling and said their name. The whole group jumps up to reflect the feeling and then crouches down to wait for the next volunteer.
- The game coordinator suggests a limited number of emotions such as happy, sad and angry. Volunteers show one of these emotions and everyone else guesses which emotion that person was showing.

Talk about

Do you ever have feelings that you don't understand or don't know why you feel that way? Do people show the same emotions in different ways? Do you ever feel happy or sad or angry just because someone else is feeling like that? Why might that happen?

Can you think of any times when it might be okay for someone to hide their true emotion from a friend? When might this have a positive effect on someone else? Can you think of times when it would not be helpful to hide an emotion?

EXPANSION ACTIVITY 14.1A. FEELINGS

As a group, think of as many feeling words as possible in 10 minutes. Write them (or draw them) on a large feelings chart on the wall. Add to this whenever anyone thinks of another word. The children choose words from the chart before and after a games session to match how they are feeling. They then share this feeling with the group (as with all games and activities, they are given the option to not contribute). (See Chapter 14, 'Group Structures for Playing IMPACT Games', in the accompanying eBook *Using Imagination, Mindful Play and Creative Thinking to Support Wellbeing and Resilience in Children*.)

EXPANSION ACTIVITY 14.1B. CATEGORIES

Paint a selection of small boxes and glue them onto a large card. The children post feeling words into the boxes according to category (for example, all the feeling words that they can think of related to 'happy'). They choose their own colours for the boxes.

EXPANSION ACTIVITY 14.1C. MATCHING

Instead of different colours, paste photographs onto the boxes showing obvious facial expressions. The children are each given a card with a feeling word on it. They take turns to try to make the same expression and then name the feeling. They then post the card into the relevant box.

EXPANSION ACTIVITY 14.2. JUST LIKE ME!

Players sit in a circle and take turns to pick an emotion card from a prepared selection that is passed around in a bowl or box. This could be a picture or a word. They name the emotion and then complete a sentence using this emotion word. For example, 'I feel happy when…' or 'I felt furious when…' Any player who has ever had the same feeling for the same reason as the speaker jumps up and shakes hands with them, or says, 'Just like me!'

Talk about

What is empathy? Do you think that we need to experience the same events as a friend in order to understand how they are feeling? Why is empathy important in a friendship?

Why might listening and observation skills be helpful for developing empathy?

15. Living pelmanism

Wellbeing focus:

☑ Self-awareness ☑ Self-reliance
☑ Self and others

Examples of personal skills learned or consolidated:

☑ Memory strategies ☑ Recognizing and understanding
☑ Tolerating frustration   emotions

Example of general/social learning:

☑ Understanding empathy

This can also be adapted as an expansion or alternative game to '11. Community skills' (for example, you could match skills and community members) and as an expansion or alternative game to '14. Feel it, do it'.

How to play

A child is chosen to be Player One. The rest of the children are paired up, or randomly assigned feeling words that go together. For example, two children could be given 'happy'. Or you could make this slightly more challenging by having words that go together, such as 'happy' and 'smile' or 'cross' and 'furious'. The children will need to be able to remember their word. They then arrange themselves randomly in a circle around Player One. Player One throws a beanbag to two others to see if they match. The catcher says their word. If there is a match, those two children sit down. Player One continues until they have found all the matches.

Adaptations

- Before Player One throws the beanbag, ask all the children to say their word three times.
- Players have their picture or written word clearly displayed in front of them

for varying lengths of time so that Player One can memorize them before they are turned over and the game starts.

• The children have their pictures/words positioned so that they are not clearly visible to the thrower but can be seen as a reminder for themselves.

Talk about

How do we recognize different emotions in other people?

How do you show that you are happy/cross/bored/disgusted?

Do you think that different people have different ways of showing the same emotion? How might you know if someone is upset? Do you think everyone gets upset about the same things?

If you knew that a friend was upset or cross about something, what would you do?

What do you like your friends to do if you are worried or upset about something?

16. If feelings were shapes

Wellbeing focus:

☑ Self and others   ☑ Self-reliance
☑ Self-awareness

Examples of personal skills learned or consolidated:

☑ Recognizing and understanding   ☑ Taking turns
emotions   ☑ Observation

Examples of general/social learning:

☑ Understanding empathy   ☑ Exploring links between
                                      thoughts and feelings

This activity and '17. Star performer' are adapted and shortened versions of two activities in *Helping Children to Manage Anger* ('23. Shaping up!' and '24. In the hot seat'). They illustrate how imagery activities can be used in a flexible way for exploring different concepts. Playing with emotion images in this way can help children to understand that they can have some control over what they feel, or over the strength of a feeling.

Note: Remind children that all images produced by members of the group are always to be accepted in a non-judgemental and respectful way. For an example of encouraging feedback in this activity, see Chapter 9, 'Image-Making', in the accompanying eBook Using Imagination, Mindful Play and Creative Thinking to Support Wellbeing and Resilience in Children.

How to play
Start by inviting the children to help make a list of positive feeling words associated with friendships or positive characteristics such as loyalty. Choose one of these to explore further.

Ask the children to settle themselves into a comfortable position in their chairs or sitting on the floor. Read the activity slowly with plenty of pauses to give them time to explore their images. Ask for feedback as appropriate.

Close your eyes and take three full breaths, letting the air out slowly as you breathe out... Feel the flow of air in and out of your body. When you are ready, move your thoughts away from your breathing...and let your imagination give you an image for [name the chosen feeling]...it might be a shape, an animal, a plant or an object...anything at all...just allow it to appear in your imagination... Now imagine that you could make this image out of modelling clay...[encourage the children to move their hands as if they were physically moulding the image into something that they could hold in their hands]... What does it look like?... Is it light or heavy?... What colour is it?... Does it make a sound? If so, what sound does it make?... If this image had a name, what name would it have?... Spend a little time playing with this image...make it bigger...and bigger...what does that feel like?... Does it have a different name when it is this size?... Make it smaller and smaller...what does that feel like?... What would you call this image now?... Mould the image back to how you would most like it to be... What would you like to do with [the image] now?

When you are ready open your eyes and give your arms and hands a shake. Stamp your feet on the ground. Now we're ready to create that!

EXPANSION ACTIVITY 16.1. CREATE THAT!

The children sculpt their own images or draw them/paint them/make up a poem about them – invite them to be as creative as they like in how they record their images.

Talk about

Can you think of some things that we might do or think that would make a feeling seem bigger or stronger? For example, if you're feeling a little bit cross, what might you do or think that would make that feeling into 'furious'? Or, if you were feeling happy, what sort of thoughts do you think would make you feel less happy? What thoughts would make you feel more happy?

Try having a different positive feeling image in each hand. What happens if you mould them together? Open your hands and just see what image emerges. What happens if you put two opposite images together? (Sometimes they simply won't mould together and sometimes they produce a third option.)

17. Star performer

Wellbeing focus:

- ☑ Self and others
- ☑ Self-awareness
- ☑ Self-reliance

Examples of personal skills learned or consolidated:

- ☑ Sharing information
- ☑ Listening
- ☑ Understanding opposites
- ☑ Answering questions

Examples of general/social learning:

- ☑ Developing dramatic awareness
- ☑ Exploring self-concept and self-efficacy

This activity links with '16. If feelings were shapes'.

Although hot seating generally involves other children in the audience asking their own questions, this exercise is best facilitated by an adult. Alternatively, the audience could be given the questions and choose which one they will each ask.

How to play

Players each choose one of the positive feeling words or characteristics from the list made in the previous activity ('16. If feelings were shapes'). They take a moment to imagine something that somehow shows what this word means. They are then invited to 'hot seat' their image as if it was a character in a story. Volunteers sit in a pre-designated chair. It is a good idea to make this a chair that is not generally used by the children. They then answer questions from the facilitator as if they were their image. So, for example, they might introduce themselves as 'I am a tree and I am called strong'. The facilitator then asks the following questions:

What size/type of tree are you? Were you always a tree or has there been a time when things were different? What do you most like about being a tree? Is there anything that you don't like about being a tree? What do you most wish for? What are you especially good at doing? What advice or suggestion do you have for your audience?

The child, having answered as many of these questions as they feel happy to, then stands up, moves away from the chair, and steps out of the image by shaking their arms and legs, hands and feet, and saying something that indicates they are back to being a child again (such as saying their own name and one thing they like to eat or what they are going to do later in the day).

The children can be encouraged to elaborate on their image as much as possible so that they have a strong sense of what their feeling or characteristic involves. If you do not have time for all the children to hot seat their image, they might do this by writing a 'character sketch' for their image as if it was going to be in an animated cartoon, or apply the characteristics to a fictitious person and write a CV outlining their suitability for a job as a football coach, for example.

Talk about

Was this activity easy or difficult? Why was that? You have heard lots of different ideas about friendships. How might these ideas be helpful to you in the future?

Could this activity be useful for exploring any other feelings?

EXPANSION ACTIVITY 17.1. THE STORIES WE TELL (3)

If you have not already done so, this could be a good time to introduce children to wellbeing stories. (See Chapter 17, 'Image-Making and Wellbeing Stories', and Chapter 18, 'Helping Children to Create Their Own Wellbeing Stories', in the accompanying eBook *Using Imagination, Mindful Play and Creative Thinking to Support Wellbeing and Resilience in Children*.)

Each child writes or tells a story based on their feeling character. They can ask to 'borrow' characters from other children, or three children could collaborate to make up a story. Remind the children that their story will need to include a helper, a task to complete or a problem to solve, one or more obstacles to overcome and a positive resolution.

The children could add their stories to their 'Book of Wisdom'.

18. Personal interviews

Wellbeing focus:

☑ Self and others   ☑ Self-reliance

☑ Self-awareness

Examples of personal skills learned or consolidated:

☑ Listening   ☑ Encouraging/reinforcing others

☑ Asking questions   ☑ Giving personal information

☑ Taking turns

Examples of general/social learning:

☑ Developing empathy   ☑ Building trust

How to play

Drape a chair with a brightly coloured blanket or cloth. The children take turns to sit in the chair and are interviewed by the rest of the group. Questions can be about their likes and dislikes, wishes, holidays, favourite books, pet hates, etc., or they can be interviewed about a particular interest they have. There is an allocated time limit for each interview. Reassure everyone that they will have a turn at being interviewed at another time if they want to be.

Adaptations

- Use two chairs, one for the person being interviewed and one for volunteer interviewers who can come and sit in the chair and ask one question before returning to their place in the audience.
- The interviewee takes on the role of a famous person or a character in a book.

Talk about

How does it feel to have the chance to talk about yourself? How does 'being interviewed' compare to having a conversation with someone? Think about taking turns in conversations and asking questions to show a genuine interest in the other person. What do you feel when a friend asks you questions about yourself?

How do you encourage someone to carry on talking or to give you more details about something? (For example, what do you say? What posture do you use? What head movement might help?)

19. Pass a gift

Wellbeing focus:

☑ Self and others   ☑ Self-reliance

☑ Self-awareness

Examples of personal skills learned or consolidated:

☑ Listening   ☑ Taking turns

☑ Giving and receiving praise

Examples of general/social learning:

☑ Building self-respect and respect for others   ☑ Exploring self-concept and self-efficacy

How to play

Use a large glitter ball or a beautiful or unusual object. Players stand or sit in a circle and pass the ball to each other (or around the group). Whoever is holding it praises someone else and passes them the ball. If you play this game regularly at the end of your times together, this is best done in sequence around the circle to start with, until you feel that the children can praise each other in random order and not leave anyone out. Encourage the children to acknowledge the praise that they are given, either verbally or non-verbally.

Adaptations

- Before starting to pass the ball, players think of several things that people could be praised for. This could be general praise or praise that is specifically related to friendships.
- The children take turns in choosing the object to be used.

Talk about

What do you feel when you give and receive praise?

How many ways can you think of to praise a friend? How do you praise yourself?

What would you most like to be praised for? What do you think your mother/father/brother/sister/best friend would most like to be praised for?

Is there anything you don't like to be praised for?

20. Follow my walk

Wellbeing focus:

☑ Self-awareness   ☑ Self-reliance
☑ Self and others

Examples of personal skills learned or consolidated:

☑ Giving and accepting   ☑ Observation
   compliments

Examples of general/social learning:

☑ Building trust   ☑ Building self-respect and respect
☑ Understanding empathy   for others
                                    ☑ Appreciating diversity

See '21. Mirror talking'.

There is a similar game in another book in this series, *Helping Children to Manage Anger* ('11. Walk this way'), where the starting point is for children to walk as an imagined character (see 'Adaptations' below). In this activity the emphasis is on mirroring each player's actual way of walking. Both games involve close observation and can lead to discussions about diversity, empathy, trust, self-respect and respect for others.

How to play

Players stand in a circle. A volunteer walks across the circle several times. The group members give positive comments about the way that the volunteer walked. For example, 'You held your head up', 'You looked well balanced', 'You smiled', 'Your shoulders were relaxed'. Then everyone tries to walk in exactly the same way and to really sense what it is like to walk like this person.

    Have as many volunteers as possible and reassure everyone that they will get a go another time if they want to.

Adaptations

- Imagine a character role and try to walk as you think they would walk, for example the strongest person in the world or someone who has just been told some good news.
- Walk in different ways to reflect different emotions.
- In pairs the children take turns to exactly mirror how their partner walks across the room.

Talk about

How does our walk express how we feel about ourselves? What sort of changes can be made to how we walk? (Such as walking with light/heavy footsteps; large strides/small steps; slowly/quickly; with a 'bounce'; arms swinging/arms stiff.)

Discuss similarities and differences in the way that people walk. How does it feel to 'walk in someone else's shoes'? How does it feel when someone else really tries to feel what it is like to be you?

In what ways does the ability to imagine help us with this game?

21. Mirror talking

Wellbeing focus:

☑ Self and others   ☑ Self-reliance
☑ Self-awareness

Examples of personal skills learned or consolidated:

☑ Understanding and using non-verbal communication   ☑ Observation

Examples of general/social learning:

☑ Understanding empathy   ☑ Building trust

How to play

Players sit facing each other in pairs. They take turns silently and slowly to move their hands, arms, shoulders and head while their partner tries to mirror their movements.

Adaptations

- Use music to evoke different moods for the movements.
- Give a theme beforehand.
- Extend to whole body movements.

Talk about

How easy or difficult was this? What skills are needed in order to follow someone else's movements in this way? What did you feel when someone else was following your movements?

22. Magic dancers

Wellbeing focus:

☑ Self and others   ☑ Self-reliance

☑ Self-awareness

Examples of personal skills learned or consolidated:

☑ Listening   ☑ Observation

☑ Self-control

Examples of general/social learning:

☑ Understanding empathy   ☑ Developing body awareness and

☑ Understanding compassion   positive body image

☑ Building trust

How to play

Player One is the 'magician'. The magician is able to cast a spell to make the children dance (with exaggerated movements) and to make them freeze. The rest of the group is divided into two halves – rescuers and dancers. Rescuers stand in a wide circle. The dancers move around the centre of the circle in time to lively music. When the magician stops the music, the dancers freeze in whatever position they are in. The rescuers take turns to exactly copy the position of one of the dancers. When a dancer thinks their rescuer has got it exactly right they are saved and can unfreeze and sit down around the edge of the group. The rescuer must then stay frozen in position until every dancer has been saved (the game coordinator may need to help some children to closely mirror positions). Then the magician has lost their powers. A new magician is chosen, the rescuers and dancers swap over, and the game starts again.

Adaptations

- Choose animals that have different ways of moving, for example snakes, birds, crocodiles (with arms stretched out to make the crocodile's jaws).
- Rescued dancers can help other rescuers.

Talk about

How easy or difficult is it to stay completely still? How easy or difficult is it to try and mirror someone else's posture? What skills did the rescuers use?

Did the dancers help the rescuers in any way?

What did you feel as a dancer? What did you feel as a rescuer?

In this game, rescuers tried to copy the dancers exactly. Do you think that a person needs to feel anger or sadness in order to understand what it is like for someone else to be angry or sad? Think of someone who is a good friend. Is it possible for you to understand what they might be feeling about something, even though you have not experienced the same thing?

What is the difference between trying to understand how someone feels and feeling sorry for them?

Can you think of some ways in which we can be kind to ourselves and to others today?

23. When being a friend is difficult

Wellbeing focus:

- ☑ Self-awareness
- ☑ Self and others

- ☑ Self-reliance

Examples of personal skills learned or consolidated:

- ☑ Listening
- ☑ Sharing personal information

- ☑ Problem-solving

Examples of general/social learning:

- ☑ Understanding empathy
- ☑ Understanding compassion

- ☑ Building trust

The discussion happens at the start of this activity. Discussions about teasing can be lengthy and I have found that the intensity of focused concentration often needs to be relieved by a simple active or 'release' game at the end. See, for example, activities '9. Big group yell' or '13. Green space group tag' in *Helping Children to Manage Anger*, another book in this series.

Talk about

Begin by asking the children to think about different ways that people tease each other, such as name-calling, taking and playing with treasured possessions, copying the way that someone walks or talks, consistently ignoring someone, and so on. Is there such a thing as 'okay teasing'? At what point does having fun together become something that is not okay?

Think about why people might tease – because they want to feel 'big', they have been teased themselves, they've just been told off, they want to be part of a 'gang', they don't understand that what they are saying or doing is hurtful, etc.

Ask for ideas about how children might respond to being teased or to seeing someone else being teased. What would happen if they responded physically? What would happen if they told an adult? They may have been told to ignore the person who is teasing, but I have never yet had a group where all the members agreed on this strategy. Many children tell me they've tried this 'but it doesn't work'. This might be because they need to come up with a way of ignoring.

Can you think of a time when you have successfully solved a difficulty in one of your friendships? Do you think that there are different ways to solve the same problems? How does dealing with teasing differ from working out disagreements with good friends?

You have heard lots of different ideas about difficulties in friendships from other children in the group. Is there anything new that you might try?

How to play

Players crouch down in a circle facing inwards. Everyone hums quietly and then gradually gets louder as they all stand up together and raise their arms above their heads. Then everyone does the reverse – starting with a loud hum and getting quieter and quieter as they sink down to the ground. Repeat this as many times as feels right. Then everyone lies down with their feet towards the centre of the circle in complete silence.

EXPANSION ACTIVITY 23.1. COPING WITH DIFFICULTIES

Complete one or all three activity sheets together (23.1a, 23.1b and 23.1c), or use one of the templates in Appendix C of the accompanying eBook *Using Imagination, Mindful Play and Creative Thinking to Support Wellbeing and Resilience in Children* to draw or write about a time when a difficult situation with friends has been successfully resolved. Add this to the 'Book of Wisdom'.

24. Sharing

Wellbeing focus:

☑ Self and others   ☑ Self-reliance
☑ Self-awareness

Examples of personal skills learned or consolidated:

☑ Problem-solving   ☑ Observation
☑ Self-control   ☑ Listening

Examples of general/social learning:

☑ Understanding empathy   ☑ Building group cohesion
☑ Understanding compassion   ☑ Understanding concept of
☑ Building trust   fairness

This game is a popular team-building/group-strengthening game for all ages. (See also '25. No/never/maybe'.)

How to play

The group is given a number of small items appropriate for the age range but not enough for everyone to have one (raisins are a good option). They are asked to come to a 'fair' decision about how the items are to be shared.

Talk about

What happened during this game? Was it easy or difficult to decide how to share fairly? Did everyone feel okay about the end result? When might sharing be important in a friendship group? When might it be important in a community group?

EXPANSION ACTIVITY 24.1. SHARING

Invite the children to work in pairs to complete or to discuss activity sheet 24.1 and then come together in the large group to talk about their ideas.

Focus on what makes sharing easy or hard and why the concept of sharing is important. Encourage the children to think about the different uses of the word 'share' and examples for things that can be 'shared' (such as ideas, conversations, special moments, worries, secrets, friends, games, meals, sweets, time, etc.).

25. No/never/maybe

Wellbeing focus:

- ☑ Self-awareness
- ☑ Self and others
- ☑ Self-reliance

Examples of personal skills learned or consolidated:

- ☑ Understanding emphasis and intonation
- ☑ Observation
- ☑ Listening

Examples of general/social learning:

- ☑ Building self-respect and respect for others
- ☑ Adaptability
- ☑ Developing dramatic awareness

How to play

The group starts by thinking of one or more requests that might cause a dilemma. For example, 'Can I borrow [a favourite or treasured possession]?'

Players stand facing each other in two circles. Those in the outer circle are 'A's. Those in the inner circle are 'B's.

Each A asks the first question. The player opposite them in the inner circle (player B) answers 'no', 'never' or 'maybe', using different intonation patterns and facial expressions. The questioner tries to guess the true meaning behind the response. Is player B being sarcastic? Are they angry? Assertive? Sad? If they guess correctly, player B then asks the same question of player A. Players can ask the question three times, but if they still can't guess the true meaning of the response, they swap anyway.

Players swap between being questioner and responder as many times as possible during one minute, giving a different type of response each time.

After one minute all players in the inner circle move one place to their right and the game starts again, with the same or a different request.

Adaptations

- Players in the inner circle (responders) move one space to the right and answer the same question in different ways until they have been all round the circle of questioners. They do this as fast as possible. Then the two circles swap places.

- Players in the outer circle make their request in different ways: 'I want...', 'Give me...', 'I will be your absolute best friend if you let me borrow...'

Talk about

What happened in this game? Was it easy or difficult to guess how the responders were feeling? Which feelings did you most enjoy acting?

Is it okay to say 'no' to a friend's request sometimes?

How do you say 'no' to an unreasonable request from a friend without sounding aggressive?

26. The house of friendship

Wellbeing focus:

- ☑ Self and others
- ☑ Self-awareness
- ☑ Self-reliance

Examples of personal skills learned or consolidated:

- ☑ Understanding metaphors
- ☑ Cooperation

Examples of general/social learning:

- ☑ Appreciating diversity
- ☑ Building self-respect and respect for others

This activity provides children with the chance to consolidate their thinking around the theme of friendships covered so far.

How to play

As a group, write down all the words about friendships that you can think of. Aim for a mixture of different aspects of friendships, including words that reflect some of the possible difficulties. Each child then draws their own 'house of friendship' and fills their picture with words that they have chosen from the joint discussion and/or new words of their own.

Join the individual houses together by threading string through them or mounting them on a wall to make a 'street of friendship'. Make smaller pictures to form a village, town or community.

Adaptation

- The children make a collaborative 'street of friendship' on a large roll of paper spread out across the room or playground.

EXPANSION ACTIVITY 26.1. THE STORIES WE TELL (4)

Make up a cooperative poem or short story about friendships. Each person contributes one word or one sentence in turn. This works well if an adult acts as scribe and reads the composition to the group when it is completed.

The rest of the expansion activities for '26. The house of friendship' involve a selection of activity sheets for you to choose from. Each of these can also be adapted for discussion or drawing according to individual and group preferences.

EXPANSION ACTIVITY 26.2. RECIPE FOR A GOOD FRIEND

Devising a 'recipe' for friendship is a well-known activity. The children can choose to be quite literal about this and have a potion of things like 'listens well', 'good at sharing', 'fun', and so on (see activity sheet 26.2).

Alternatively, this is a chance to explore the imagination even more and go wild with the potion ingredients! For example, one seven-year-old put an iguana, mud, a frog and chocolate cake among his ingredients!

EXPANSION ACTIVITY 26.3. WHAT MAKES A GOOD FRIEND?

The aim with activity sheet 26.3 is to help children to think more about what a person can do to *form* friendships as well as to identify why it is that they get on with a particular friend.

This could lead to a discussion about having friends who are different from each other. For example, two very different children might be friends with a third child but not particularly close friends with each other. Encourage the children to think why that might be.

The difference between 'being popular' and 'being a good friend' could also be discussed with the group if appropriate (see 'Expansion activity 26.4' and 'Expansion activity 26.5.).

EXPANSION ACTIVITY 26.4. ONE OF MY FRIENDS

I suggest that the children are given a choice about which activity sheet to complete, 26.4a or 26.4b. It is also important that they are encouraged to choose a friend who is not part of the group. This avoids the possibility of a popular child or a child with a large friendship group being chosen by several group members while others are not chosen by anyone.

'Important' information can be written around or inside the magic mirror, such as 'likes toffee', 'ace at mending things'.

EXPANSION ACTIVITY 26.5. SPECIAL FRIENDSHIP DAY

Use activity sheet 26.5a and/or activity sheet 26.5b according to the needs and stage of the group. Talk about the differences and similarities in the children's ideas for special friendships.

Cooperation and Negotiation

By doing the activities in this section you will be helping children to:

- continue to build or consolidate self-respect and respect for others
- build or consolidate skills of cooperation and negotiation
- build or consolidate their ability to share responsibility for group effectiveness and problem-solving.

27. Blindfold obstacle course

Wellbeing focus:

- ☑ Self and others
- ☑ Self-awareness
- ☑ Self-reliance

Examples of personal skills learned or consolidated:

- ☑ Focusing attention
- ☑ Giving instructions

Examples of general/social learning:

- ☑ Understanding responsibility
- ☑ Building trust

How to play
One player is blindfolded and must navigate their way over an obstacle course relying on verbal instructions given by one or more of the other players.

Adaptation

- Work in pairs, with the 'seeing' partner walking next to the player who is blindfolded.

Talk about
Is it easy or difficult to give instructions to someone who is blindfolded?

Is it easier to give instructions to one person or to a group?

Do you feel more comfortable giving instructions or following instructions?

What goals are you working towards at the moment? Are there any obstacles in your way? How might friends help each other to overcome difficulties?

28. Green space music

Wellbeing focus:

- ☑ Self and others
- ☑ Self-awareness

- ☑ Self-reliance

Examples of personal skills learned or consolidated:

- ☑ Understanding feelings
- ☑ Taking turns
- ☑ Observation
- ☑ Sequencing

- ☑ Listening
- ☑ Self-control
- ☑ Memory strategies
- ☑ Physical coordination

Examples of general/social learning:

- ☑ Understanding teamwork and leadership skills

- ☑ Building group cohesion

This activity requires some preparation by the facilitator who will need to collect various natural objects so that children can make musical instruments, such as rainsticks. These can be made from a large piece of bamboo cane with sand or grit inside and sealed at both ends. You could also make thunder makers. These are rigid cardboard tubes closed at one end with something that will vibrate like velum on a drum. A long spring is attached to the closed end (so that it is hanging outside the tube). When it is shaken it vibrates and echoes round the tube, like thunder.

Music-making in a band or orchestra is a powerful means for promoting pro-social behaviour and numerous personal skills. There has been much research that suggests that active music-making as part of a group helps children to express their emotions, enhances their listening and coordination skills, improves language skills and decreases aggressive behaviour. We also know that being in green spaces, and in particular being mindful when in green spaces, can have positive effects on our sense of general wellbeing. Combining these two aspects (hopefully without scaring the wildlife!) can be fun and energizing for all concerned.

How to play

Players start by making a variety of instruments from natural objects, They then compose outdoor orchestral and solo performances to convey different emotions, different seasons or conflict and conflict resolution scenarios. The game coordinator demonstrates how to 'conduct' an orchestra with hand movements that indicate, for example, loudly/softly, quickly/slowly, all join in, stop. Players stand in a row, in small groups or in a circle according to the size of the group. Conductors take turns to conduct the orchestra as a whole group and with duos, solos, etc.

Adaptations

- Instead of musical instruments, players make different sounds from nature such as a bird call, the buzz of a bee, etc.
- Combine instruments and sounds from nature.
- Use movements instead of sounds, for example hop, jump, stretch, wave.

Talk about

What does it feel like to be the conductor? What does it feel like to be part of the orchestra? What are some of the difficulties involved in being a conductor? What does it feel like to do a solo or duo when you are part of an orchestra?

Do all games need a leader? Is 'leading' the same as coordinating? Do friendship groups sometimes have 'leaders'? Why is this? Do community project groups have leaders? Why is this? What are some of the skills that leaders/coordinators might need?

29. Big bugs

Wellbeing focus:

- ☑ Self and others
- ☑ Self-awareness
- ☑ Self-reliance

Examples of personal skills learned or consolidated:

- ☑ Observation
- ☑ Giving instructions

Examples of general/social learning:

- ☑ Understanding teamwork and leadership skills
- ☑ Building trust

How to play

Players form a large 'centipede' by holding on to each other around the waist or placing their hands on the shoulders of the person in front of them. The centipede walks around a large obstacle course. Everyone keeps their eyes shut except the person at the front who has to lead them safely through and give instructions as they go, keeping careful track of what is happening to all parts of the centipede.

Adaptations

- Drape a parachute over the line of players to make a big centipede or a dragon. One player stays outside to give directions or holds the end of the parachute above their head so they can see where they are going. They then lead the centipede or dragon around a large open space.
- Make trains and coaches with a driver at the front.

Talk about

What does trust mean? Did you trust the centipede leader/train driver to give you the right instructions? Can you think of a time when a friend has given you some good ideas about how to handle a difficult situation? Has there ever been a time when someone has trusted you to do something? How did that feel?

30. Towers

Wellbeing focus:

- ☑ Self and others
- ☑ Self-awareness
- ☑ Self-reliance

Examples of personal skills learned or consolidated:

- ☑ Problem-solving
- ☑ Taking turns
- ☑ Cooperation

Examples of general/social learning:

- ☑ Reducing impulsivity and building persistence
- ☑ Understanding teamwork and leadership skills
- ☑ Adaptability
- ☑ Understanding that there can be more than one solution to a problem

How to play
Groups of children cooperate to build the highest tower possible with a selection of materials such as cardboard, drawing paper, masking tape and tissue paper.

Adaptation

- The children cooperate in silence to complete the task.

Talk about
What worked? What didn't work? Why was this?
    Is it easy or difficult to work silently as a group?
    How did you communicate with each other? Did everyone have the chance to contribute? Why? Why not?

31. Working parts/team machine

Wellbeing focus:

- ☑ Self-awareness
- ☑ Self and others
- ☑ Self-reliance

Examples of personal skills learned or consolidated:

- ☑ Cooperation
- ☑ Negotiating
- ☑ Problem-solving

Examples of general/social learning:

- ☑ Understanding teamwork and leadership skills
- ☑ Understanding the value of individual contributions for group success

How to play

Small teams (around five is a good number) think of a machine that has several working parts. Each member of the team takes on the role of a different part in the machine (and an 'operator'). Players can use sounds and actions and have parts working together or at different times.

Each team practises their machine and then demonstrates it for the other teams to guess what it is.

Adaptations

- Teams pick a machine from a prepared set of cards.
- Teams invent a machine and explain it to the rest of the group.

Talk about

Did all team members take an equal part? Is it possible for teams to be non-competitive? Did teams have a leader or did all members join in with the decision-making?

32. Abandon ship!

Wellbeing focus:

- ☑ Self and others
- ☑ Self-awareness
- ☑ Self-reliance

Examples of personal skills learned or consolidated:

- ☑ Negotiating
- ☑ Compromise
- ☑ Cooperation
- ☑ Problem-solving

Examples of general/social learning:

- ☑ Building self-respect and respect for others
- ☑ Adaptability
- ☑ Focusing on common goals

How to play

The children are split into an equal number of small groups or pairs, according to the size of the whole group. Within each group, members imagine that they are on a ship that is about to sink. They have a lifeboat, but they are only allowed to take 10 items with them from the ship. First they think of 10 items each. They then negotiate with other team members as to what to take as they can only take 10 items between them. Groups then join with another group and renegotiate the 10 items. Eventually the whole group meets and negotiates a final list of 10 items.

Adaptation

- The whole group has been shipwrecked. They have two empty plastic bottles to use on the desert island. Small groups or pairs think of as many uses as possible for the two bottles. The whole group then pool their ideas.

Talk about

How did this feel? Is everyone happy with the final decision? How easy or difficult was it to agree on 10 items? What are some of the benefits of working in a group to solve problems?

33. Where shall we go?

Wellbeing focus:

- ☑ Self and others
- ☑ Self-awareness
- ☑ Self-reliance

Examples of personal skills learned or consolidated:

- ☑ Negotiating
- ☑ Compromise
- ☑ Cooperation
- ☑ Problem-solving

Examples of general/social learning:

- ☑ Developing sensitivity to other people's strengths and differences
- ☑ Understanding concept of inclusion
- ☑ Focusing on common goals

How to play

The children are split into an equal number of small groups or pairs, according to the size of the whole group. Players imagine that they are a 'holiday' committee. They have been given the task of planning a day out for the whole group. They must take into consideration any special requirements of group members and must negotiate an agreed day out that they think will cater for everyone's likes and dislikes. After 10–15 minutes each committee chooses a spokesperson to present their ideas to the rest of the larger group. Further discussion and negotiation should be encouraged in order to reach an agreement between all players.

Adaptation

- Committees plan an afternoon of entertainment for someone else, for example the residents of a local care home or a group of younger children.

Talk about

See 'Talk about' for 32. Abandon ship! What skills did you need for this task? Being an effective negotiator isn't about getting your own way. Sometimes it involves reaching a compromise or helping others to come to an agreement.

87

34. Uses for a beanbag

Wellbeing focus:

- ☑ Self and others
- ☑ Self-awareness
- ☑ Self-reliance

Examples of personal skills learned or consolidated:

- ☑ Problem-solving
- ☑ Taking turns
- ☑ Observation
- ☑ Summarizing information

Examples of general/social learning:

- ☑ Understanding teamwork and leadership skills
- ☑ Exploring self-efficacy

How to play

Players divide into teams and are given materials to make their own beanbag, for example from socks filled with dried beans. They need to ensure that the sock is securely tied and is not too full or too loosely packed. Each team then thinks of as many different things that their beanbag could be used for in a given environment – for example, in a classroom, at home, in a science lesson or in a zoo.

After a set time, the teams get together to share their ideas and make a joint list. They then go back to their own team to think of one new idea that isn't on the list.

Each team discusses what happened during this game, and then chooses one person to summarize their discussion for the large group. A selection from the 'Talk about' section below could be used as prompt questions for the discussion.

Adaptations

- Have a selection of different weights and sizes of beanbag. Discuss different uses for different bags.
- Teams think of at least one idea that can be demonstrated (for example, a door stop).

Talk about

Is it easier for you to think of ideas in a group or on your own? Why is this?

Is it easier for you to take your time to think about things slowly or to think quickly? Why is this?

Did you have the chance to say all your ideas? Did other people have some of the same ideas as you?

What happened when you went back to your group to think up one last idea?

Celebrating Together

These activities provide an opportunity for recapping and celebrating. There are therefore no suggestions for personal skills learned or consolidated.

You might also give time for children to vote for a favourite game to play – just for fun!

35. All yours

How to play

Players divide into teams or pairs and review a selection of the games already played. Each team identifies at least five skills or strategies that they have discussed or learned while playing these games. They then construct a short role-play about two or more children who use these skills to resolve their conflicting ideas about how to complete a task or help a friend who is being teased. Teams take turns to demonstrate their role-play to the whole group.

Adaptations

- Increase the number of required skills and strategies.
- Increase or decrease the time limit for the initial discussion.
- Combine elements of each team's role-play to make a longer play.
- Change the conflict situation to a disagreement between two characters from a novel who can't agree on how the book should end.
- Teams could concentrate on a particular skill such as effective listening but demonstrate what might happen when these skills are not used. For example, showing disinterest by using inappropriate facial expressions and body language, interrupting, changing the topic, not asking any questions or asking too many questions, avoiding eye contact, etc.

Talk about

This could be an opportunity for one or more children from each team to lead the discussion in the same way that a director might participate in an audience Q & A session after the screening of their film, or a panel of experts might respond to questions about a documentary.

36. Inner expert

How to play

Use the imagination tent (from '6. Imagination tent') as a 'Find the expert' room.

Players make a joint list of questions that they would like to ask an expert about friendships. They each choose one question. They then go through one end of the tent to meet their expert. They imagine themselves speaking to this expert and asking their question. They then imagine themselves becoming the expert.

They sit for 10 seconds in the middle of the tent and imagine themselves becoming an expert in friendships, really feeling what that is like. As the expert, they respond to the question and then go back to being themselves again. They then emerge from the other side of the tent with their expert knowledge. What is their best 'tip' about friendships that they would like to share with the group?

In larger groups you might want to ask for a limited number of volunteers for this, or use one of the methods for choosing the order of play outlined in Chapter 14, 'Group Structures for Playing IMPACT Games', in the accompanying eBook *Using Imagination, Mindful Play and Creative Thinking to Support Wellbeing and Resilience in Children*. Since it is likely that most children will want to go through the tent eventually, this is a good activity to revisit several times. As the group evolves, the changes in 'expert' advice may act as a useful indicator of how children are progressing in their understanding of friendship and community skills.

37. Closing circles

Everyone sits in a circle and says one thing that they feel good about.
For example:

> I feel...
>
> I found out that...
>
> Today I felt...
>
> My name is _____ and I am...
>
> I have noticed that...
>
> I feel really good about...
>
> My next step is...
>
> I want to say that...
>
> Today this group has given me...

Wait until all group members have had a turn (including adult facilitators), and then everyone applauds themselves and each other as loudly as possible.

VII

Activity Sheets

The activity sheets in this section can be adapted for discussion or used as a basis for devising more complex activity sheets for older children.

Where possible, I suggest that you encourage children to draw rather than to write, and to work together rather than to sit quietly completing activity sheets on their own. This sharing and talking will not only help to foster collaborative, mutually respectful relationships; it also offers an opportunity for each child to enrich their understanding of the benefits of using imagery, being mindful and thinking creatively.

ACTIVITY SHEET 1.1. MY NAME STORY

What do you know about your name? Write about or draw your name story here:

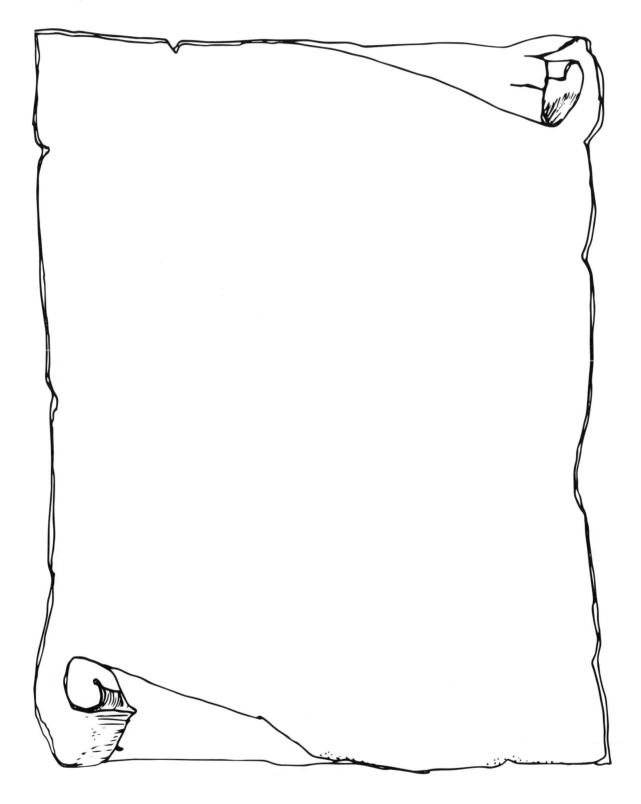

ACTIVITY SHEET 2.1. WISDOM RULES!

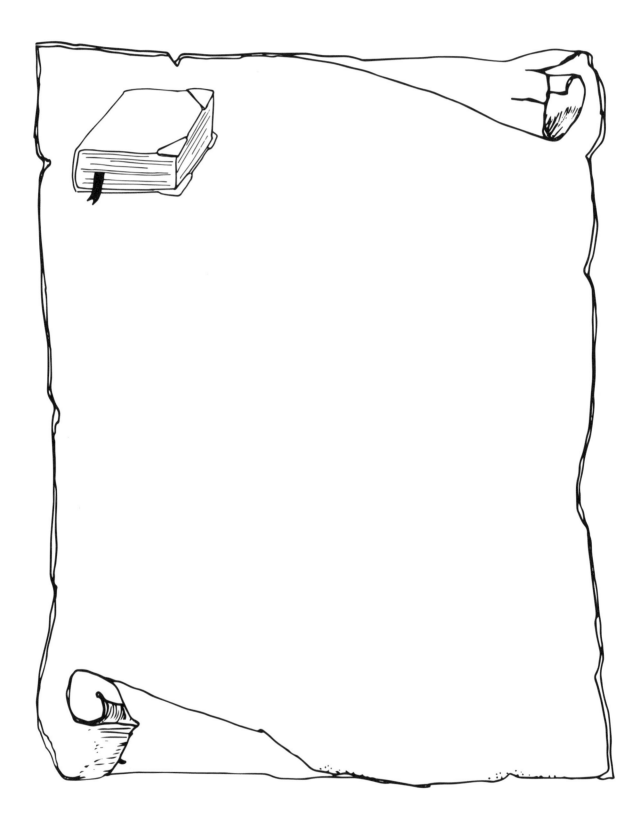

ACTIVITY SHEET 8. GETTING TO KNOW YOU

Find as many people as possible in the group who can agree with the following statements:

I own a bicycle (and I use it).

I have a pet.

I enjoy watching sport.

I have seen one of my favourite films more than three times.

I like spicy food.

It took me more than one hour to get here today.

I play a musical instrument.

I have an unusual hobby.

I don't like chocolate.

ACTIVITY SHEET 8.1A. DESCRIBING PEOPLE

These are some words that I can use to describe people:

....

....

....

....

I can describe how they look (tall, brown eyes, curly hair):

....

....

....

....

....

....

I can describe what they are like (happy, thoughtful):

....

....

....

....

ACTIVITY SHEET 8.1B. MY GROUP

Write down everyone's name in your group. How do you think they would like to be described? Write one friendly describing word next to each name:

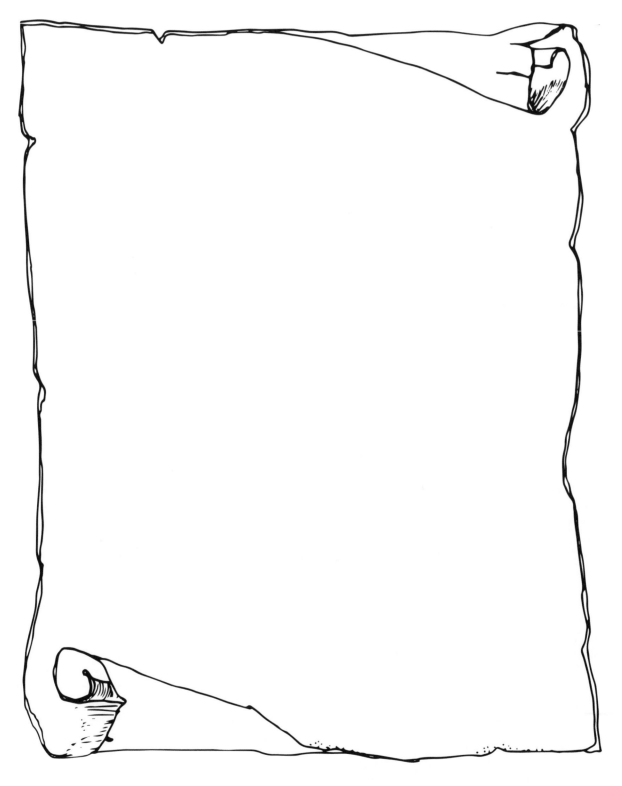

ACTIVITY SHEET 23.1A. WHEN BEING A FRIEND IS DIFFICULT

Let's say you and one of your friends disagree about something. Imagine that your friend has come to your house for tea. Your friend wants to play outside and you want to play indoors with a new game that someone has given to you. How does that feel? What might happen?

....
....
....
....
....

Imagine that it is time for your friend to go home now and you didn't manage to sort out the disagreement. How do you feel? What happened? What did you do? What didn't you do?

....
....
....
....
....

Now imagine that your friend is going home and you did manage to sort things out. You both feel okay. What happened? What did you do? What did you say?

....
....
....
....
....

ACTIVITY SHEET 23.1B. TEASING (1)

Let's spend a little time thinking about something that is not a friendly thing to do. Have you ever been teased?

What is teasing? Think of all the different ways that someone might tease another person.

....

....

....

....

....

....

Think about why people might tease.

....

....

....

....

....

....

ACTIVITY SHEET 23.1C. TEASING (2)

How does it feel to be teased? Think of as many words as you can to describe what people might feel like when they are teased.

....

....

....

....

Now let's think of some things that you could do.

If I was being teased I could...

....

....

....

....

If I saw someone else being teased I would...

....

....

....

....

I would not...

....

....

....

....

ACTIVITY SHEET 24.1. SHARING

What does the word 'sharing' mean?

....

....

....

....

Imagine that you've just had a birthday and you've been given some special pencils for drawing. You take them into school to use when you do your work. Would it be okay to share them or would that be difficult for you?

It would be okay to share them if...

....

....

....

....

It would be hard for me to share them if...

....

....

....

....

What other things can be shared?

....

....

....

....

ACTIVITY SHEET 26.2. RECIPE FOR A GOOD FRIEND

Imagine that you have a book full of magic recipes. The very first recipe in the book is how to make friends. What do you think the magic potion will be made of?

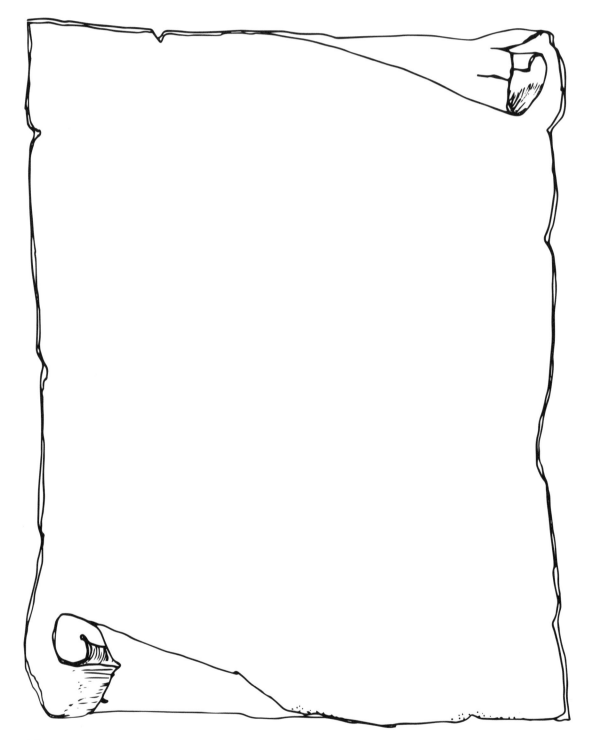

Now you are giving your imagination a good work out!

ACTIVITY SHEET 26.3. WHAT MAKES A GOOD FRIEND?

_____ is a good friend because...

....

....

....

....

Some things we like doing together are...

....

....

....

....

One of the nicest things I have ever done for a friend is...

....

....

....

....

ACTIVITY SHEET 26.4A. INTRODUCING MY FRIEND

Imagine that you are your best friend talking about themselves. What would your friend say? For example, what might they say about what they like doing and what they are good at?

What might they say about what they don't like doing and about what worries them? Begin with their name:

_____ is...

ACTIVITY SHEET 26.4B. ALL ABOUT MY FRIEND

Imagine that one of your friends could look into a magic mirror. What would they see? What would your friend say was important about who they are? Draw a picture of your friend in the magic mirror.

107

ACTIVITY SHEET 26.5A. SPECIAL PERSON FOR THE DAY

Imagine that it's your special friendship day. Everyone is going to be extra-friendly today. They want to know what you like friends to do so that they can be sure to get it right. What will you tell them?

....

....

....

....

I like it when my friends...

....

....

....

It is not friendly to...

....

....

....

ACTIVITY SHEET 26.5B. MY SPECIAL FRIENDSHIP DAY

Imagine that it is the end of your special friendship day and you have had a wonderful time with everyone being extra-specially friendly.

What did you do together? What did you do that helped the day to go well? What were you like with your friends? (For example, were you relaxed? Smiley?) How did you feel? What do you feel now? Close your eyes and just imagine…

When you are ready, draw or write about your special day here.